LEARNING THAT LASTS

A GUIDE FOR HEALTH PROFESSIONS STUDENTS
WHO WANT TO MAXIMIZE THEIR LEARNING

THOMAS GUS ALMONROEDER, PT, DPT, PHD

CONTENTS

PREFACE

My motivation for writing this book is simple. I want to help students, particularly health profession students, succeed academically and get the most out of their educational experience. Training to become a healthcare provider is hard, regardless of the discipline. There's a lot to know and the expectations are high. That said, during my years as an educator I've never worked with a student who didn't have what it took to be successful academically. In most cases, it seems that students struggle because they don't have a solid plan when it comes to their learning. My hope is that this book can be a helpful resource for these students who are struggling, as well as for those who simply want to maximize their learning.

I wrote this book from the perspective of a former student and experienced educator. As a student, I didn't always use the best study strategies. As is usually the case, I wish I'd known then, what I know now. Much of what I discovered about the science of learning occurred after I had already completed my formal education. Although it may be too late for me (at least as far as being a student), I've made it my mission to share what I've learned along the way, so that students like you can get the most out of your education.

HOW THIS BOOK IS ORGANIZED

This book is generally divided into three sections: Chapters 1 and 2 review some fundamental concepts of learning and explain how students can benefit from changing the way they study, Chapters 3-9 introduce six evidence-based study strategies and describe how to put them into action, and the remaining chapters discuss additional ways to maximize your learning (e.g. effective note-taking, how to read a textbook).

While I discuss the evidence and theoretical basis for different study strategies throughout this book, I don't go into much depth. This book isn't meant to be a deep dive into educational psychology or the science of learning. My goal was to create a resource that's evidence-based, but also easy to read and filled with useful tips.

ACKNOWLEDGEMENTS

Writing a book takes careful planning and persistence. It also takes lots of support and encouragement. I'm very lucky to have such a great team to help me along the way. It starts with my family. My wife Sarah provided words of encouragement as I developed this book and feedback on early drafts. I'm blessed to have such a wonderful partner. My daughter Grace and son Jack provided inspiration and needed mental breaks throughout the writing process. Whenever I was stuck, I could count on them to make me laugh and take my mind off this project.

Besides my family, I'd also like to acknowledge a couple colleagues who provided support and helpful feedback. Tricia Widenhoefer is a colleague of mine at Trine University. Everyone should be lucky enough to work with someone like Tricia. This book wouldn't have come to fruition without her words of encouragement and thoughtful feedback. Cameron Buzzard was also a great source of support for this project. Cameron is a physical therapist and former student of mine. He and I have worked together to create a "study strategies" course for health professions students, which covers much of what's discussed in this book. Cameron provided excellent ideas and helpful feedback throughout the writing process. It's great to be able to work with someone like Cameron who is such a natural when it comes to working with students.

Finally, I'd like to thank my current and former students. I'm very lucky to work with such talented, committed, and hard-working people. Your efforts and persistence inspire me to continue striving to become a better teacher. You deserve my best.

CHAPTER 1

EMBRACING THE SCIENCE OF LEARNING

The *science of learning* involves studying how people learn in order to develop evidence-based approaches that teachers and students can use to maximize learning. The science of learning builds upon research from various fields, including cognitive psychology and neuroscience. Although it's a relatively new field of study, learning scientists have already improved our understanding of effective teaching and learning practices, while also helping to dispel certain myths about learning.[1]

Despite these advances in the science of learning, students often adopt study strategies based on their own assumptions about how learning works or their sense of what seems to be effective. Unfortunately, the strategies most students use don't align with what's been shown to be optimal for learning based on research. This is a missed opportunity for students to reach their full learning potential.

As a student, you'll want to make sure you're using study strategies that have been shown to maximize learning. In essence, that's what this book is mainly about – introducing you to evidence-based study strategies and explaining how you can incorporate them into your studying routine. These aren't tricks or "hacks" to make learning easy. Meaningful learning takes time, commitment, and lots of hard work. There aren't any shortcuts. However, by leveraging the science of learning, you can get the most out of the time and effort you put into studying.

Before moving forward, it's important to understand what I mean by *learning*. Learning isn't about being able to memorize facts or definitions for a short period so you can regurgitate them for an exam. Meaningful learning is achieved when the knowledge and skills you've gained are long-lasting and can be applied in the future. This type of "durable" learning is particularly critical for health professions students, who will eventually need to be able to apply knowledge and skills from their training when working with patients.

Health professions students also need to learn in a manner that will allow them to apply knowledge and skills to new situations. It's unrealistic to think that your training will equip you with the precise knowledge and skills needed for every situation you'll encounter as a healthcare provider. Therefore, your learning needs to be somewhat "flexible", so that you can translate your basic knowledge and skills to novel situations.

The study strategies discussed in this book are those that have been shown to promote the type of durable and flexible learning that you'll need to be successful throughout your career.

HOW STUDENTS TYPICALLY STUDY

Study strategies can be broadly categorized according to the level of cognitive processing they involve. Passive studying approaches involve consuming information through reading or listening, with minimal attempts to engage with the material. Re-reading lecture notes is an example of a passive approach. With these types of passive approaches, the assumption is that repeated exposure to information will lead to learning. Unfortunately, this turns out to be a flawed assumption. In contrast, active studying approaches involve greater levels of cognitive processing, as learners engage with content. Activities like attempting to explain concepts from memory, coming up with real life examples, or mapping out the connections between different concepts are examples of more active studying approaches, since they involve relatively high levels of cognitive processing (vs. more passive activities like re-reading lecture notes).

When surveyed, college students typically report spending a large proportion of their study time on relatively passive approaches, like reviewing lecture notes or re-reading the textbook.[2,3] However, research indicates that active approaches are much more effective for learning.

How students study isn't the only issue – timing also matters. Students often report studying for long periods of time, shortly before their exam (so called "cramming"). During these sessions they'll typically focus on one topic, essentially trying to burn it into memory. However, research tells us that this approach isn't conducive to long-term learning.

These discrepancies between what students typically do and what we understand to be best practices for learning based on research offer opportunities for improvement. If you can learn to leverage the science of learning you can organize your studying in a manner that will lead to better long-term learning outcomes.

WHY STUDENTS TEND TO USE SUBOPTIMAL STUDY STRATEGIES

It's interesting to consider why students tend to gravitate toward relatively ineffective study strategies. One reason is that strategies that are suboptimal for learning often feel highly effective in the moment (i.e. while you're studying). Conversely, strategies that are more effective in the long-term often feel less effective. In other words, what's good for your learning in the long-term seems to be ineffective in the moment. I'll elaborate on this idea more later in the chapter.

Another reason is that studying strategies often get "handed down" to some extent. What I mean is that students often get ideas for how to study from their peers. Sometimes these ideas are sound; however, most times they aren't. For example, the program I teach in has students organized into cohorts. Second-year students in our program will often speak with incoming students about how they "survived" their first year of graduate school. I've listened in on these sessions in the past. In many cases second-year students offer really great advice; however, when it comes to study strategies, student advice doesn't always align with what we know to be optimal for learning. Admittedly, instructors can also be sources of poor advice. While this advice is certainly well-intentioned, it can end up perpetuating myths and misconceptions about learning.

AVOIDING ILLUSIONS OF COMPETENCE

One major challenge we face as learners is that strategies which seem to be effective in the short-term often result in suboptimal learning outcomes. What I mean is that while certain activities, such as re-reading lecture notes, may promote immediate improvements in our ability to recall, or at least recognize, information, these short-term gains don't tend to translate into longer term learning. In other words, approaches that seem to be highly effective while we're studying, don't actually end up being very effective in the long term. As learners, we generally don't have an accurate sense of what's good for our learning.

For instance, one of my go-to approaches as a student was to read over my notes multiple times, often in a single session (usually the night before the exam). I'd find a comfortable spot in the library, load up on coffee, and repeatedly re-read my notes over and over again, until the library closed for the night. It felt like an effective approach, since I became more and more familiar with my notes each time I passed over them. However, this familiarity gave me a false sense that I'd mastered a topic and would be able to retrieve the information when I needed it, such as during an exam or when working with a patient.

Unfortunately, the gains I made during my study sessions were often temporary, as I'd forget much of what I'd reviewed, usually within the next couple days. I also struggled to apply course concepts. Even if I could recite a definition or parrot an example my instructor had used in class, I'd struggle when asked to apply what I'd studied. In the end, what I thought to be a reflection of learning, was really just familiarity with my notes. I was suffering from an "illusion of competence", where I wrongly assumed that familiarity with my lecture notes or other course materials was a sign that I understood and could apply what I had studied. Sadly, my illusion of competence usually came crashing down as soon as I was asked to move beyond simple short-term memorization.

Despite my shortcomings, I always did well enough to pass my classes. That said, I wasn't getting the outcomes I wanted. I often felt like I wasn't retaining much of what I'd learned and I struggled to apply course concepts. To my credit, I at least had enough sense to realize that I needed a new approach. This is what prompted me to become interested in the science of learning. I wanted to get more out of my efforts.

When I began teaching, I noticed that my students often used the same study strategies I'd used, with similar results. After a subpar exam, they'd come to my office explaining how they'd studied for hours, but what they'd studied just didn't seem to stick. They'd say things like, *"I went over my notes dozens of times and knew the information, but for some reason my mind went blank during the exam."* The reality was that these students had been fooled by the same illusion of competence that had plagued me as a student. They assumed that familiarity with their notes was a reflection of learning. Sadly, it's not.

When I'd ask students what they planned to do to improve their performance on the next exam, they'd typically tell me that they'd double down on their studying efforts. If 20 hours of studying for the exam wasn't enough, they'd try 40 hours. I'd then explain that their poor exam performance probably wasn't related to a lack of time and effort. Instead, it was likely due to the faulty (albeit common) way they studied. In most cases students don't need to study longer, they just need to study "smarter", for lack of a better term.

EMBRACING DESIRABLE DIFFICULTIES

In general, learning activities that require a considerable amount of cognitive effort promote long-term learning. Dr. Robert Bjork, a professor in cognitive psychology at the University of California, Los Angeles, coined the term *desirable difficulties* to describe this idea.[4] Dr. Bjork used the term "desirable difficulties" to highlight that what feels difficult while we are studying often leads to desirable learning outcomes in the future. In contrast, approaches that offer minimal challenge, often aren't very effective in the longer term, even though they lead to good immediate performance and feel effective in the moment.

As an example, consider passively re-reading notes versus attempting to recall information from memory. Re-reading notes is obviously much easier, since it doesn't involve the mental effort required to retrieve information from memory. All you need to do is recognize what's written on the page. However, there's strong evidence that actively recalling information from memory (referred to as *retrieval practice*) leads to better long-term retention, compared to re-reading. Therefore, efforts to recall information from memory should be viewed as a desirable difficulty; it's hard in the moment and you may not always be successful when studying (we can learn a lot from mistakes), but the added mental effort will lead to better long-term learning. The same is true when it comes to varying the topics or the types of problems you're working on when studying. In the moment, it feels easier, and we tend to be more successful, when we focus on a single topic or problem type. However, research suggests that we learn more when we mix up the topics we're studying or the problem types we're working on (referred to as *interleaving*). These are just a couple examples of approaches that feel arduous while we're studying, but ultimately lead to better learning outcomes (i.e. desirable difficulties).

When considering desirable difficulties, it's important to understand that just because something makes studying hard, doesn't mean it's good for your learning. For example, if you're trying to study, but are distracted by a noisy roommate, this presents a difficulty, but not one that's likely to improve your learning (i.e. it's a difficulty that's not desirable). The same is true when you attempt challenges that are way beyond where you're at as a learner. For example, if you're new to a topic it may not be possible to generate your own examples of how concepts could be applied. Eventually you'll want to get there, but it may hinder your progress if you attempt this level of challenge before you're ready. Desirable difficulties offer a sufficient challenge, but at a level that's appropriate for where you're currently at as a learner.

An analogy I like to use with students is that studying is like going to the gym. You need to challenge yourself at a level that's sufficient to promote positive changes, but not to the point where what you're trying to do is far beyond your current capabilities. For example, if you go to the gym and repeatedly lift really light weights (whatever "light" means for you), it won't be challenging enough to stress your muscles in a manner that will make them stronger. On the other hand, if you try to lift a weight that's well beyond what you could even think about lifting, that's not going to do you much good either (it's difficult, but not in a way that's likely to help you get stronger). You need to find a balance between what's challenging enough to help you improve, but not so challenging that you don't have a chance to be successful, regardless of your efforts. Then you can progressively increase the level of challenge over time, as your knowledge builds.

The focus of this book will be on discussing study strategies that offer the type of cognitive challenges that will lead to better learning outcomes. By "better" I mean strategies that will help you store and retrieve information from long-term memory, understand how concepts relate, and apply what you're learning to your day-to-day life. I'll also discuss ways that you can tailor different strategies to align with where you're at as a learner. In the end, your goal should be to find a "sweet spot" where you're appropriately challenged when studying.

LEARN TO THINK LIKE A SCIENTIST

One piece of advice I often give students is to begin thinking like a scientist when it comes to their learning. What I mean is that they should be willing to try different approaches and conduct their own self-experiments to see what works best for them. The reality is that you probably won't go through your entire educational experience without a few poor exam performances along the way. It happens. However, one bad exam grade shouldn't be viewed as a failure. Instead, it's a data point that you can learn from and use to revise your approach. If something isn't working, make some changes to your studying routine and see if your performance improves. Essentially, turn a bad exam into good data.

A key here is to understand that your perception of what's effective while you're studying probably isn't a good gauge for whether you're learning. As we've discussed, we can be fooled quite easily, especially if we aren't using sound study strategies. That said, use more objective data points, such as your exam scores, to inform your plan of action.

It's also important to realize that what works for one course or topic may not work well for another. Or what worked well for you at one point in your learning process may stop working. Like a scientist, you need to continuously re-evaluate with each new data point and adjust accordingly.

It's also worth noting that you don't need to completely revamp your entire approach all at once. Pick a couple new strategies, try them out, and evaluate your performance. If they work, great! If not, revise your approach and re-evaluate.

Thinking like a scientist can be quite liberating, since the goal is to continuously improve your process, not necessarily to ace every exam. It also aligns with the idea of adopting more of a "growth mindset" where setbacks or suboptimal performance are viewed as opportunities for growth, instead of signs that you don't have what it takes to be successful (i.e. more of a "fixed mindset").[5]

FINAL THOUGHTS

As I've discussed in this chapter, students typically opt for study strategies that aren't necessarily optimal for their learning, such as passively re-reading their lecture notes or other course materials. By leveraging the science of learning you can identify better approaches that will promote the types of desirable difficulties that are conducive to meaningful, long-term learning.

It's important to understand that learning requires cognitive effort. Studying should feel hard; if it doesn't you probably aren't doing it optimally. Our brain isn't like a sponge that passively soaks up and holds information. You need to mentally wrestle with information and ideas in order for them to stick. Otherwise, what you review will tend to get lost in the endless stream of information you're exposed to – here today, gone tomorrow.

REFERENCES:

1. Weinstein Y, Madan CR, Sumeracki MA. Teaching the science of learning. *Cogn Res Princ Implic.* 2018; 3(1): 2.

2. Karpicke JD, Butler AC, Roediger HL. Metacognitive strategies in student learning: do students practise retrieval when they study on their own? *Memory.* 2009; 17(4): 471-479.

3. Piza F, Kesselheim JC, Perzhinsky J, et al. Awareness and usage of evidence-based learning strategies among health professions students and faculty. *Med Teach*. 2019; 41(12): 1411-1418.

4. Bjork RA. Chapter 9: Memory and metamemory considerations in the training of human beings. In: Metcalfe J, Shimamura AP, eds. *Metacognition: Knowing About Knowing*. MIT Press; 1994: 185-205.

5. Dweck CS. *Mindset: The New Psychology of Success*. Random House; 2006.

CHAPTER 2

AN INTRODUCTION TO BLOOM'S TAXONOMY

Before starting to discuss specific study strategies, I'd like to introduce you to Bloom's Taxonomy, which is a framework used to describe different levels of knowledge mastery. Bloom's Taxonomy was first described in 1956 by educational psychologist Benjamin Bloom and his colleagues, as a way to categorize course learning objectives.[1] While it's undergone some revisions throughout the years,[2] the basic concept and core elements have remained the same.

Within Bloom's Taxonomy, there are six hierarchical categories that describe different levels of learning, progressing from remembering (lowest level) to creating (highest level) (Figure 2.1). Bloom's Taxonomy is well-known among educators, as it can serve as a useful guide for planning lessons and assessing student learning. However, most students aren't familiar with Bloom's Taxonomy, which can make it difficult for them to effectively plan their studying and gauge their level of mastery of a topic. As a student, you'll benefit tremendously from having a basic understanding of Bloom's Taxonomy.

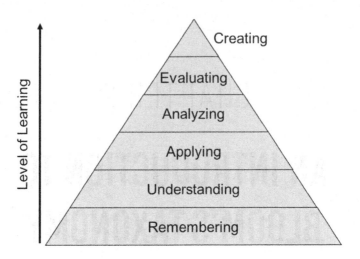

Figure 2.1. Levels of Bloom's Taxonomy, progressing from *remembering* (lowest level) to *creating* (highest level).

A CLOSER LOOK AT BLOOM'S TAXONOMY

Now, let's take a closer look at each level of Bloom's Taxonomy, starting with the most basic level and progressing to the most advanced level.

Level 1 - Remembering

Remembering involves recognizing or recalling information from memory. At this level, learners have memorized definitions, facts, or basic concepts verbatim, without really understanding them. This is the lowest level of learning since it essentially just involves parroting back information.

Level 2 - Understanding

Understanding is where a learner has reached a level where they can explain something in their own words, as they begin to realize the meaning of what they've learned. A student at this point has moved beyond rote memorization. However, understanding is still considered a relatively low level of mastery, since learners still aren't able to apply what they've learned.

Students are often surprised that understanding is considered a relatively low level of learning, since they often assume that they've mastered a concept if they can explain it. However, it's important to note that just being able to explain something doesn't mean you recognize how it could be applied or how it relates to other concepts or pieces of information.

Level 3 - Applying

Applying is where learners can use information in new situations to solve problems. This is where learning starts to become meaningful to some extent, as a student at this level is able to put what they've learned to use.

Level 4 - Analyzing

Analyzing is where learners can perform an in-depth examination of what they've learned. A student at this level is able to break down information into its basic components and understand how these components relate to one another. They can also make connections, seeing the "bigger picture" of how information and concepts are related.

Level 5 - Evaluating

Evaluating is where learners can make judgements about ideas, theories, or problem-solving approaches. A student at this level would be able to do things like compare two approaches and determine which is most likely to be effective, based on their knowledge of the different approaches.

Level 6 - Creating

Creating is the ultimate level of mastery, where learners can use what they know to come up with new theories, processes, and so on. At this level, an individual's level of mastery has progressed to the point where they can push the boundaries of what's known or possible.

Levels 1 and 2 of Bloom's Taxonomy (*remembering* and *understanding*) are generally considered low levels of learning, while levels 3-6 (*applying, analyzing, evaluating,* and *creating*) are considered higher levels of learning, since they involve much deeper levels of cognitive processing.

Now, let's consider a specific example of how learning outcomes differ across the levels of Bloom's Taxonomy. Imagine you're studying pharmacology and learning about different medications. At level 1 (*remembering*) you would be able to do things like list the different classes of medications. At level 2 (*understanding*) you would be able to explain how different types of medications work. At level 3 (*application)* you would be able to do things like select an appropriate medication based on a patient's condition. Levels 4 (*analyzing*) and 5 (*evaluating*) would involve even higher levels of mastery, allowing you to do things like identify factors that may impact the effectiveness of a certain medication or determine the most appropriate medication from a set of options. Finally, level 6 (*creating*) would involve something like coming up with an idea for a new medication based on your deep understanding of a disease process and principles of pharmacology.

As a student, you may not be expected to reach the creating level of Bloom's Taxonomy (unless you're involved in research or something along those lines). However, I'm sure you can already appreciate why it's important for health professions students to be able to move beyond memorization and basic understanding.

WHY STUDENTS SHOULD UNDERSTAND BLOOM'S TAXONOMY

As I've mentioned, Bloom's Taxonomy is widely known among educators, but less so among students. So, you may be asking yourself why it's important for students to be familiar with Bloom's Taxonomy. I think there are a few good reasons.

First, it's important to understand what's expected of you as a student. Does your instructor just expect you to memorize definitions and to be able to generally describe basic concepts? Or are they expecting you to be able to do things like apply course concepts or compare different theories or processes? If you don't know, it's important to find out so you can make sure you're studying in a manner that will allow you to reach the target level of learning. Students often get caught off guard when they're first asked to move beyond remembering and understanding.

You can get an idea of what's expected by reviewing the course learning objectives, which are usually in the syllabus. These objectives will tell you what you're expected to be able to do after completing the course. If you see verbs like "define", "list", "describe", or "identify" in the learning objectives, your instructor may not expect you to be able to achieve higher levels of learning. This is often the case for introductory courses, where you'll build upon your basic level of knowledge in subsequent courses. However, if you see verbs like "apply", "differentiate", "compare", "appraise", or "develop", it should be a signal to you that you're expected to move to higher levels of learning. Table 2.1 includes examples of action verbs associated with each level of Bloom's Taxonomy.

Table 2.1. Examples of action verbs associated with each level of Bloom's Taxonomy

Level	Verbs
Remembering	Define, label, list, name, recognize, recall
Understanding	Explain, describe, summarize, classify, discuss, translate
Applying	Solve, use, demonstrate, show, execute, perform
Analyzing	Compare, break down, differentiate, organize, distinguish, relate
Evaluating	Appraise, judge, defend, critique, rank, recommend
Creating	Design, construct, plan, develop, produce, formulate

Another reason to be familiar with Bloom's Taxonomy is that it can help you to continuously push yourself to achieve higher levels of learning. For example, if you feel comfortable explaining a concept, try to identify different ways the concept could be applied or try to relate the concept to others you've discussed in class. These efforts to push yourself to higher levels of learning will help you to expand and deepen your level of knowledge. As you read about the different study strategies in this book, try to consider how you could use them to progress to higher levels of Bloom's Taxonomy.

Finally, I think understanding Bloom's Taxonomy can help you speak a common language with your instructor. Instructors often highlight the importance of developing "critical thinking skills", without really explaining to students what this means. If you understand Bloom's Taxonomy, you'll begin to realize that what they mean is that you need to get to a point where you can analyze, evaluate, and problem-solve, not just memorize and explain.

MOVING BEYOND THE COGNITIVE DOMAIN

What I've presented in this chapter is related to the cognitive domain of Bloom's Taxonomy. However, it's important to note that similar hierarchies exist for the affective and psychomotor domains. It may be worth exploring these other domains if you're interested in progressing your affective or psychomotor skills, which are also critical for health professions students.

FINAL THOUGHTS

What I've presented in this chapter is a very general overview of Bloom's Taxonomy; there's certainly much more to learn. That said, having a general understanding of Bloom's Taxonomy will help you to more effectively align your study strategies with your target learning objectives. It also provides you with a framework for progressing to increasingly higher levels of learning. Remember, learning is a journey, without a final destination.

REFERENCES:

1. Bloom BS. *Taxonomy of Educational Objectives, Handbook 1: Cognitive Domain*. David McKay Company, Inc. 1956.

2. Anderson LW, Krathwohl DR. *A Taxonomy for Learning, Teaching, and Assessing: A Revision of Bloom's Taxonomy of Educational Objectives.* Longman. 2001.

CHAPTER 3

RETRIEVAL PRACTICE

If You Can't Remember, It's Time to Recall

Have you ever been in a situation where you knew the information you needed was stored in the deep recesses of your brain, but just couldn't seem to pull it forward? Of course you have, otherwise you wouldn't be reading this book. This used to happen to me all the time, and still does more often than I'd like to admit. In most cases it was during an exam. I'd stare at a question, knowing I'd reviewed the slide with the exact information I needed dozens of times, but for some reason I couldn't access it when it mattered. I'd re-read the question over and over again until the last few minutes of the exam period, hoping my brain would clear the cobwebs. Sadly, it never seemed to happen in time.

This situation always bothered me. It didn't necessarily hold me back from passing my classes (I still did fairly well), but I hated to get questions wrong when I had studied the material. No matter how much I studied, I knew I'd run into a couple questions that stumped me. I also noticed how little I retained between classes. It felt like I was starting all over again whenever a topic was revisited.

When I started teaching, I noticed that a lot of my students had the same issues. So, I started looking into how people can get better at storing information in their memory and retrieving it when needed. While I wasn't taking exams anymore, I wanted to be able to help my students.

While reviewing the literature, I realized that much of the problem was related to the way students tend to study. In most cases, students spend a vast majority of their time passively re-reading their notes, over and over again, essentially trying to force-feed their brain information.[1,2] I'm not judging. This was also my go-to approach as a student. The problem is that this approach doesn't involve retrieving information from memory and applying it, which is what most exams are all about (professors don't really care if you can recognize their slides). If you want to be able to retrieve information during exams (or when a patient asks you a question, which is probably more critical) you need to practice recalling information and applying it. Every retrieval attempt, whether successful or not, strengthens the neural pathways involved in storing information and retrieving it from memory. There's some strong science to back this up, as key areas of the brain involved in memory become active when you attempt to recall information.[3]

The focus of this chapter is on *retrieval practice* (also commonly referred to as *active recall*), which involves attempting to retrieve information from memory to promote learning. There's tons of research on the topic of retrieval practice. It's been shown to strengthen memory of facts, concepts, processes, and problem-solving approaches, which are all things you'll need to remember as a student and future clinician. You'll want to figure out how to make retrieval practice a regular part of your study routine, if it isn't already.

A LOOK AT THE LITERATURE

As I've mentioned, there's lots of research on the topic of retrieval practice. However, I'd like to highlight one study by Drs. Henry Roediger and Jeffery Karpicke that I find particularly interesting.[4] Drs. Roediger and Karpicke published their study back in 2006, while working at Washington University in St. Louis. In their paper they describe two experiments they conducted with college students to examine how attempting to recall information from memory impacts knowledge retention.

Experiment #1

In their first experiment, Drs. Roediger and Karpicke asked students to read two short passages. One of the passages was about the sun, the other was about sea otters, although I'm not sure that's relevant. Then, after a short break, the students were asked to either review the passage again (analogous to what students do when they review their notes a second time) or to try to recall as much information as they could about the passage by writing what they remembered on a blank piece of paper (a form of retrieval practice). To test the students' retention, Drs. Roediger and Karpicke examined the number of key concepts students could remember from both passages after 5 minutes, 2 days, and 1 week.

Roediger and Karpicke's findings are shown in Figure 3.1. After 5 minutes, the students recalled 81% of the information they had read and then reviewed (study-study condition) and only 75% of the information they had read and then attempted to recall (study-recall condition). While these results indicated that studying the material twice led to better short-term retention, the longer-term outcomes told a different story. After 2 days, the students only recalled 54% of the information they had studied twice, compared to 68% of the information they had studied once and then attempted to recall. The results after 1 week showed a similar pattern, with students recalling 42% of the information they had studied twice versus 56% of the information they had studied once and then attempted to recall.

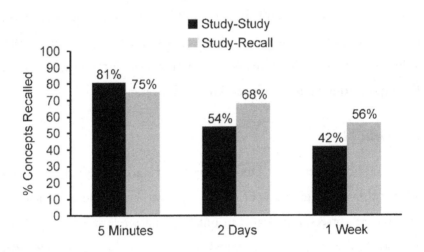

Figure 3.1. Percentage of key concepts recalled from the passages (% concepts recalled) 5 minutes, 2 days, and 1 week after the initial session, when students studied the passage twice (study-study) and when they studied the passage once and then attempted to recall the information (study-recall).

Clearly, studying the passage once and then attempting to recall was better for longer-term retention, compared to studying the passages twice. In fact, the students recalled more information after 1 week in the study-recall condition than they did after 2 days in the study-study condition (56% vs. 54%), which is pretty amazing. The other interesting thing to note is that the students didn't even receive any feedback after their recall attempt. The simple act of trying to retrieve information from memory was enough to promote better long-term retention.

Experiment #2

In their second experiment, Drs. Roediger and Karpicke expanded on their original work and had students study a passage four times (study-study-study-study condition), study a passage three times and then attempt to recall the information once (study-study-study-recall condition), or study a passage once and then attempt to recall the information three times (study-recall-recall-recall condition), with short breaks between the study-recall periods. Like the first experiment, they examined the number of key concepts students could remember after intervals of 5 minutes and 1 week.

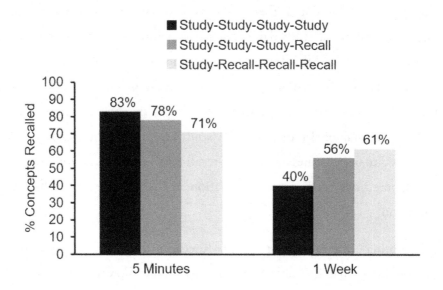

Figure 3.2. Percentage of key concepts recalled from the passages (% concepts recalled) 5 minutes and 1 week after the initial session, for each condition (study-study-study-study, study-study-study-recall, study-recall-recall-recall).

Roediger and Karpicke's findings for the second experiment are shown in Figure 3.2. After 5 minutes, students recalled 83% of the information they had studied four times (study-study-study-study condition), 78% of the information they had studied three times and then attempted to recall (study-study-study-recall condition), and only 71% of the information they had studied once and then attempted to recall three times (study-recall-recall-recall condition). In general, these results indicated that more time spent reviewing the passages corresponded with better short-term retention.

However, as was the case in their first experiment, the longer-term outcomes were flipped. After 1 week, students recalled 40% of the information they had studied four times, 56% of the information they had studied three times and then attempted to recall, and 61% of the information they had studied once and then attempted to recall three times. These results showed that longer-term retention became better as students made more recall attempts. Again, these findings are pretty amazing. Especially when you consider that, on average, the students re-read the passages a total of 14 times in the study-study-study-study condition, compared to only 3 times in the study-recall-recall-recall condition, yet they remembered over 20% more information in the study-recall-recall-recall condition.

Another interesting aspect of Roediger and Karpicke's second experiment is that they asked students to predict how well they would perform on the 1-week retention test. Students expected to perform best in the study-study-study-study condition, even though this ended up being the condition where they performed worst. This may provide a clue as to why students tend to adopt a strategy where they repeatedly review their notes over and over. It feels like an effective approach. Even though this appears to be an illusion of competence, where students falsely assume that familiarity with their notes is an indicator of learning.

While Drs. Roediger and Karpicke's work provides insights into the potential usefulness of retrieval practice as a learning activity, it's reasonable to question whether their findings generalize to "real-life" situations where students are preparing for an actual exam. I realize that not many of your classes will involve studying passages about the atmospheric conditions of the sun or the dietary habits of sea otters (not that those aren't interesting topics). That said, retrieval practice has been shown to be associated with superior learning outcomes for a wide range of topics, in a number of different contexts. For instance, Dr. John Dobson and his colleagues found that retrieval practice promoted better knowledge retention of skeletal muscle anatomy, which is a topic that's highly relevant to most (probably all) health professions students.

RETRIEVAL-INDUCED FACILITATION

It's worth noting that attempting to recall information may facilitate learning of related concepts, beyond those that were specifically recalled.[6-8] This phenomenon is generally referred to as "retrieval-induced facilitation".

For example, imagine that you are preparing for a physiology exam by taking a practice test (which can be a great activity for retrieval practice). One of the questions on the practice test asks about the mechanism of action of a certain neurotransmitter. Attempting to recall information to answer this question about the mechanism of action of the neurotransmitter may help to reinforce your knowledge of how the action of the neurotransmitter is terminated, since these concepts are related. It's as though you subconsciously review material stored adjacent to what you're trying to recall.

Although the underlying mechanisms of retrieval-induced facilitation aren't well understood, we can certainly make use of the fact that the benefits of retrieval practice appear to extend beyond the specific information being retrieved from memory. I like to think of it as getting a little added return for your efforts.

ACTIVITIES THAT INVOLVE RETRIEVAL

Now, let's discuss some activities you can incorporate into your studying routine that involve retrieving information from memory.

Write what you know from memory

This is exactly what Drs. Roediger and Karpicke had the students in their experiment do. Just select a topic (it can be specific or more general), grab a blank piece of paper, and write down everything you can remember. You can think of this as a "brain dump" of sorts. Once you've written everything you can remember, go back to your notes and see what you missed. Later, you can revisit the topic and try again. Remember, additional retrieval attempts will help to reinforce information into your memory. The key here is not to rely on your notes.

Students often tell me that they rewrite their notes as a form of studying, essentially copying what they've already written during lecture. To be clear, this probably won't be nearly as effective as writing what you know from memory. Rewriting your notes isn't great for promoting retention since it doesn't require any form of active recall. Remember, your brain doesn't function like a sponge, soaking up information it's exposed to. It really needs to be working hard for information and concepts to stick. I'll often ask students if they watch TV or listen to music while they are rewriting their notes. In most cases they say they do. This is a clue that rewriting notes doesn't require much mental effort. If you don't need to focus, the activity probably isn't challenging enough for much learning to occur. Re-writing notes word-for-word is also inefficient since it takes so long. There are certainly better ways to spend your studying time.

Answer questions about the material

Testing is typically thought of as a form of assessment, where an instructor evaluates what you know about a topic. However, it's also a great learning activity. This shouldn't come as a surprise, since answering questions from memory requires you to recall information, which generally promotes retention (often referred to as the "testing effect").

The challenge can be to find or create practice questions. Some instructors will provide practice questions. Otherwise, you can usually find them online or in the back of your textbook. You can also easily turn learning objectives into questions.

Writing and then answering your own questions can also be very beneficial. I've found that writing questions during a lecture is a great way to stay engaged and then I have something to test myself on later. The questions you use for studying don't need to necessarily be high quality. They just need to be good enough to prompt you to retrieve information from memory.

It's worth noting that short answer questions tend to be better for studying than multiple choice questions, since short answer questions require you to recall information, not just recognize a correct response.[9]

Explain concepts to someone else, from memory

There's an adage that the best way to learn something is to teach it. Why is this true? Probably because teaching requires you to retrieve information from memory and organize it in a manner that others will understand.

This doesn't need to be anything formal. Just find a classmate, friend, family member, or really anyone who will listen and explain whatever you're trying to learn, without looking at your notes. If there's nobody available, you can talk yourself through the concepts.

Teaching others is an activity that I've found very helpful for my own learning. I find that it's easy for me to identify gaps in my own knowledge when I attempt to explain things to others. And yes, there have been times when I've identified these gaps in my knowledge in the middle of class. It's slightly embarrassing, but definitely a learning opportunity for both me and my students.

It can also be helpful to try explaining concepts at different levels. For example, you can practice explaining a concept like you're teaching someone who knows little about the topic. This will force you to focus on the most important concepts, without relying on technical terms and jargon. This is not only great for learning but is also good practice for when you start working with patients.

You can also have your partner ask questions as you explain a concept or process, which is sometimes referred to as a "nosy friend approach". For example, if you tell your nosy friend that a signal passes from a neuron to a muscle fiber, they'll ask "how?". This will force you to stop and explain this intermediate step in the process. If they stump you, you've identified something to review later. It's better to identify these gaps in your knowledge when studying, as opposed to when you're in the middle of an exam.

Use flashcards, the right way

Students often like to use flashcards for studying. Flashcards can be a good learning tool, but students often don't use them optimally. In most cases students look at the definition and then try to recall the term. Instead, flip the flashcard over, look at the term, and then try to explain what it means. This requires a greater level of understanding and recall.

Also, make sure you avoid the temptation to turn the flashcard over before you've attempted to recall the answer. This really defeats the purpose of flashcards.

Occlude labels on visuals

Instructors often rely on figures or diagrams to explain key concepts, especially in courses like anatomy and physiology. Blocking out the labels on these figures and then attempting to recall them is a great form of retrieval practice. You can also occlude axis labels and/or the figure legend to see if you can still explain what the figure represents without them. If you understand a concept, you should be able to determine what the lines on a graph represent, even without these labels. I use this as an in-class review activity quite often and have found it to be very useful.

What I've presented here is certainly not an exhaustive list of options. There are many other activities that promote active recall. All it takes is some creativity.

FINAL THOUGHTS

If you only take one thing from this book, I hope it's that a big chunk of your study time should be devoted to retrieval practice. It really is remarkably effective for learning.

It's also important to understand that activities which involve retrieval will feel really challenging, as they require considerable amounts of cognitive effort. Much more than relatively passive activities like re-reading your notes. This type of effort is good for learning (i.e. a "desirable difficulty"). Remember, your brain is kind of like a muscle; it needs to be challenged in order to become stronger. If your study sessions feel challenging, you're probably on the right track. If not, you're probably not going to retain much.

You should also be aware that you likely won't be able to recall much when you first start studying a topic, which is okay. Your performance while you're studying isn't what's important. Learning is a process that needs both time and effort.

REFERENCES:

1. Karpicke JD, Butler AC, Roediger HL. Metacognitive strategies in student learning: do students practise retrieval when they study on their own? *Memory*. 2009; 17(4): 471-479.

2. Piza F, Kesselheim JC, Perzhinsky J, et al. Awareness of usage of evidence-based learning strategies among health professions students and faculty. *Med Teach*. 2019; 41(12): 1411-1418.

3. Wiklund-Hornqvist C, Stillesjo S, Andersson M, Johsson B, Nyberg L. Retrieval practice facilitates learning by strengthening processing in

both the anterior and posterior hippocampus. *Brain Behav.* 2021; 11(1): e01909.

4. Roediger HL, Karpicke JD. Test-enhanced learning: taking memory tests improves long-term retention. *Psychol Sci.* 2006; 17(3): 249-255.

5. Dobson JL, Perez J, Linderholm T. Distributed retrieval practice promotes superior recall of anatomy information. *Anat Sci Educ.* 2017; 10(4): 339-347.

6. Chan JCK, McDermott KB, Roediger HL. Retrieval-induced facilitation: initially nontested material can benefit from prior testing of related material. *J Exp Psychol Gen.* 2006; 135(4): 553-571.

7. Cranney J, Ahn M, McKinnon R, Morris S, Watts K. The testing effect, collaborative learning, and retrieval-induced facilitation in a classroom setting. *European Journal of Cognitive Psychology.* 2009; 21(6): 919-940.

8. Oliva MT, Storm BC. Examining the effect size and duration of retrieval-induced facilitation. *Psychol Res.* 2023; 87(4): 1166-1179.

9. McDaniel MA, Anderson JL, Derbish MH, Morrisette N. Testing the testing effect in the classroom. *European Journal of Cognitive Psychology.* 2007; 19(4/5): 494-513.

CHAPTER 4

SPACED PRACTICE

It's Not Just How You Study, But Also When

If I had a nickel for every time I was told not to "cram" for a test while I was a student, I'd be rich (not that I always heeded this advice). It's something we're continuously told throughout our education. The reality is that cramming, or studying in one long session shortly before an exam (e.g. the night before), is a solid strategy for improving our immediate knowledge of a topic. It may even help you score well on an exam. However, cramming is extremely poor for promoting long-term knowledge retention. What you learn from cramming is typically very temporary – often disappearing within a few days' time or less.

The type of studying students do when they cram is a form of "massed practice", where materials are reviewed in one long, continuous session. This is in contrast with "spaced practice" (also referred to as "spaced repetition" or "distributed practice"), where studying is spread across several sessions, spaced out in time. For example, imagine a student who studies a total of 6 hours for an exam. Massed practice would involve completing all 6 hours of studying in one long session. However, if they divided their studying into four 90-minute sessions (still 6 total hours), spread out over the weeks leading up to the exam, this would be an example of spaced practice.

Spaced practice has been shown to be much more effective than massed practice for promoting long-term retention of information, concepts, and skills (generally referred to as the "spacing effect"). I'd argue that this type of long-term retention is particularly important for health professions students for several reasons. First, your classes tend to build on one another, with instructors expecting you to know information from prior classes. For instance, you need to know quite a bit about physiology and pathophysiology in order to understand pharmacology. Second, most students entering a health profession will eventually need to pass some type of comprehensive board exam in order to practice. These types of exams require you to demonstrate your knowledge and deep understanding of topics covered throughout your training, necessitating long-term retention. Finally, and most importantly, healthcare providers need to be able to remember vast amounts of information so they can apply it when working with their patients. As future healthcare providers, you're not just studying to pass an exam. Your real tests will come with each and every patient encounter. This requires you to learn in a manner that won't easily fade over time.

The focus of this chapter is on *spaced practice*, which essentially involves breaking up studying into smaller chunks, spread out over time. It seems simple, but it does require some careful planning. That said, efforts to incorporate spaced practice will not only help to improve your long-term retention but could also improve the efficiency of your studying (i.e. similar or better outcomes, with less time studying).

LEARNING AND THEN FORGETTING

The story of spaced practice begins with the work of a German psychologist named Dr. Hermann Ebbinghaus, who pioneered the scientific study of memory starting in the late 1800s. Dr. Ebbinghaus's work was groundbreaking at the time and is still referenced frequently in psychology. In fact, studies are still being conducted to replicate and better understand his work.[1] Dr. Ebbinghaus truly was a pioneer in memory research and experimental psychology.

Dr. Ebbinghaus conducted a series of experiments, with himself as the test subject, where he examined his ability to remember what he referred to as "nonsense syllables".[2] Nonsense syllables are one syllable, consonant-vowel-consonant combinations, like "jom" or "gud". They are similar in structure to actual words, but don't have any meaning. Dr. Ebbinghaus used these nonsense syllables, instead of regular words, so his prior knowledge wouldn't influence his learning and retention (use of nonsense syllables became pretty common in memory research after Dr. Ebbinghaus's work). In his experiments, Dr. Ebbinghaus would study ordered lists of nonsense syllables until he had memorized them. Then he would test his ability to recall the lists at different time intervals, ranging from 20 minutes to over 30 days.

One of Dr. Ebbinghaus's most well-known findings was that forgetting tends to occur very rapidly at first and then tapers off over time, usually after a day or so. His observations led to what has been described as the "forgetting curve". Figure 4.1 depicts the typical pattern of the forgetting curve. A couple things to note are that much of what we initially study/memorize will be forgotten over time and that forgetting tends to occur very rapidly at first (starting almost immediately). Although the slope of the forgetting curve depends on what we are attempting to learn (some things are easier to retain than others), the general pattern holds true. Dr. Ebbinghaus's work helps to highlight that, although forgetting can be frustrating, it should be viewed as a natural phenomenon.

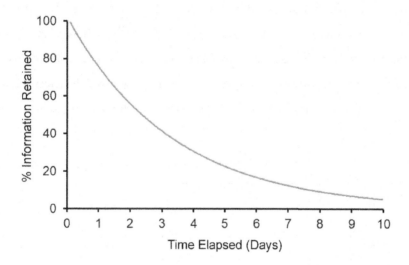

Figure 4.1. Depiction of the forgetting curve, where the Y-axis represents the percentage of information an individual can remember (% information retained) and the X-axis represents the time from when they first learned it (time elapsed).

The rapid forgetting that tends to occur after initially learning something should make it clear why "cramming" is so ineffective for long-term retention. While massed study sessions may help us remember something in the short-term, much of what we learn will fade rapidly if it isn't revisited.

Interrupting forgetting

While much of what we initially learn will be forgotten, we can interrupt forgetting by reviewing at a later time (i.e. spaced practice). For example, reviewing a day after you initially learned something will not only help you relearn it, but will also slow subsequent forgetting. This process repeats each time we review, until a point (hopefully) where what we are attempting to learn has become durable in our long-term memory and is no longer quickly forgotten. This is where we want to get to as learners. Figure 4.2 shows how repeatedly reviewing over time can impact forgetting.

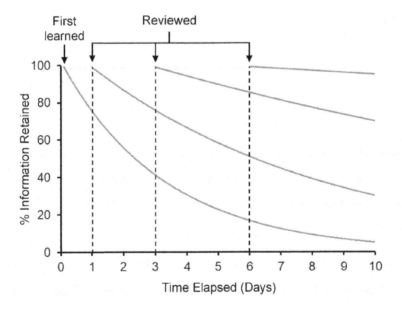

Figure 4.2. Figure showing how reviewing materials at spaced time intervals can interrupt forgetting. In this case, forgetting is very slow after the third review (occurring on day 6). Also notice the progressive increase in time between each review session.

It's also worth noting that because the rate of forgetting decreases each time we re-learn something, a greater time delay can occur between successive review sessions. For instance, while the optimal time to review may be within 24 hours after first learning something, the next review session can be extended out farther (e.g. 2-3 days later). This process continues until information very rarely needs to be reviewed. In other words, the frequency in which you need to review tends to fade over time, as the information becomes more deeply entrenched in your long-term memory.

The key is for review sessions to be appropriately spaced over time, with the goal of finding the "sweet spot" where some forgetting has occurred, but not so much that it's like completely starting over. This point where we have forgotten some, but not all, of what we've learned is when we want to review.

It's also important to note that I use "review" very generally here. Approaches that involve active retrieval, such as those described in Chapter 3, will likely lead to better retention than more passive approaches, like simply re-reading your notes.

THE EFFECTS OF SPACED PRACTICE ON LEARNING

As we've discussed, forgetting is a natural phenomenon, which can be disrupted (or at least slowed) by spaced practice. Now, let's review some examples of how the so-called "spacing effect" has been used to promote improved student learning outcomes.

First, let's discuss a study by Dr. Price Kerfoot and his colleagues from Harvard Medical School.[3] They published a paper back in 2007 describing how they used weekly educational emails to promote knowledge retention of key urology concepts.

Dr. Kerfoot et al.'s study included third-year medical students who completed online tutorials related to four topic areas in urology during a 1-week urology clinical rotation. The topic areas were prostate cancer, screening with prostate-specific antigen (PSA), benign prostatic hyperplasia, and erectile dysfunction. The students were randomly assigned to receive weekly educational emails related to two of the four topics: either prostate cancer and PSA screening or benign prostatic hyperplasia and erectile dysfunction. The weekly emails included a short, clinically relevant, multiple-choice question, with an explanation of the correct answer. The goal of providing these regular educational emails was to give students the opportunity for regular review (including retrieval practice) of the urology concepts they had previously learned.

Dr. Kerfoot and his colleagues examined students' performance on a urology exam taken at the end of the academic year. They broke student performance down according to whether they had received educational emails related to the topics, or not. For both topic sets, students who received the weekly educational emails outperformed those who hadn't, on the end-of-year urology exam. These findings indicated that providing students with opportunities to periodically review key urology concepts (a form of spaced practice) helped to promote long-term knowledge retention. The students also reported that they found the weekly educational emails to be an effective educational tool. For once, students liked something that was good for their learning!

I highlight this study by Dr. Kerfoot and his colleagues because it's an excellent example of how retrieval practice and spaced practice can be blended to promote better knowledge retention. Opportunities for retrieval, spaced out over time, is a great recipe for learning.

While Dr. Kerfoot's work focused on knowledge retention, there is also evidence suggesting that spaced repetition can help with retention of psychomotor skill learning. For instance, Dr. Edward Spruit and his colleagues published a paper in 2014 describing how spaced repetition could be used to promote more effective laparoscopic surgical skill training.[4] As part of their study, two groups of medical students trained by practicing various skills needed to perform laparoscopic surgery. Both groups trained for a total of 225 minutes; however, one group completed all training in a single day (massed practice group), while the other groups' training was broken into three separate 75-minute sessions, one week apart (spaced practice group). The students' laparoscopic surgical skills were assessed 2 weeks and 1 year after they completed their training.

At both the 2-week and 1-year follow-up time points, the students in the spaced practice group outperformed those in the massed practice group, in terms of speed and accuracy when completing a simulated laparoscopic suturing task. The students in the spaced practice group were also much more likely to achieve proficiency in performing different laparoscopic skills, compared to those in the massed practice group. These findings indicate that even though the groups completed the same amount of training, spacing out the training over multiple sessions led to better surgical skill learning. In other words, the students who participated in the spaced practice training got a better return on their time investment.

As noted by Dr. Spruit and his colleagues in their paper, teaching clinical skills, such as suturing, is often done in a single massed session. This is mainly for the sake of convenience. However, that doesn't mean you can't make spaced practice part of your personal routine for learning clinical skills.

WHY IS SPACED PRACTICE EFFECTIVE?

There are quite a few different ideas as to why spaced practice is more effective than massed practice for promoting long-term retention. Some believe that spaced practice tends to be better because it involves more active recall, since we need to retrieve relevant information from memory with each new session. This contrasts with massed practice where we can largely rely on information stored in our working memory. Others believe it may be because massed practice tends to lead to greater mental fatigue and less ability to focus. Anecdotally, I can certainly attest to the fact that my ultra-long cramming sessions left my brain feeling fried. Still others point to the fact that spaced practice provides opportunities for sleep between sessions, which appears to be critical for memory consolidation.[5]

In the end, it's probably some combination of these factors (and others) that give spaced practice the edge over massed practice.

HOW TO BUILD SPACED PRACTICE INTO YOUR ROUTINE

Now that we've discussed some of the benefits of spaced practice, let's consider how you can effectively space out your studying to optimize your learning.

First and foremost, it's important to do whatever you can to avoid needing to cram. In most cases, this involves carefully crafting a study plan that specifies when you'll review different materials. I realize this can be challenging when you're juggling multiple classes. That said, the upfront time spent developing a study plan will likely pay off in the long term.

This doesn't need to be overly complicated. It can be as simple as working backward from an upcoming exam to sketch out when you'll review certain materials to ensure that you've flattened out your forgetting curve in time. Or maybe your plan involves devoting a certain portion of your study time to revisiting older material (e.g. 20% older material, 80% new material). This is also a good way to mix up your sessions, which can also be effective for learning (see Chapter 5 on interleaving).

The good news is that in most cases you won't need to spend too much time reviewing, since re-learning something tends to occur more rapidly than initially learning it (a concept generally referred to as "savings").

As I mentioned earlier in the chapter, the key is to find the "sweet spot" with respect to timing out when to review material. Again, you want to review at a point where you've forgotten some, but not all, of what you previously learned. If you find that you remember most or all the information pertaining to a certain topic, put it aside for a longer period before reviewing again. You probably won't remember it forever, but you've bought yourself some time.

If you want to take your studying to another level, there are software solutions that can automatically adjust when you review certain information. For example, Anki is an intelligent digital flashcard application that recognizes how well you know a topic and adjusts accordingly, ensuring that weaker concepts get revisited more frequently (https://apps.ankiweb.net/). It's very useful for incorporating optimal spacing into your studying routine (Anki also has other features that make it a great learning tool). I recommend trying it out. Especially since it's free for most users and works across different devices and platforms. There are also other applications, such as RemNote, that offer similar functionality.

Although I mentioned this earlier in the chapter, I think it's worth repeating that I'm using the term "review" very loosely here. When you revisit information you previously learned, you should still rely heavily on the types of active learning activities described in Chapter 3, which involve retrieval from memory. Simply re-reading your notes or re-watching lecture videos are not great strategies, even if they're perfectly timed out.

FINAL THOUGHTS

As you can see, it's not just *how*, but also *when* you study that impacts your learning. Therefore, it's important to build spaced practice into your studying routine.

It's also important to remember to give yourself some grace. You'll learn things, forget them, relearn them, and forget them again over time. It's part of a continuous cycle of (re-)learning-forgetting that we all experience. That said, don't be ashamed of forgetting things and needing to refresh from time-to-time. It's just the way it is. Our brains have finite storage capacity. To forget is to be human.

REFERENCES:

1. Murre JMJ, Dros J. Replication and analysis of Ebbinghaus' forgetting curve. *PLoS One*. 2015; 10(7): e0120644.

2. Ebbinghaus H. *Memory: A Contribution to Experimental Psychology*. Teachers College Press; 1913. (English translation of Ebbinghaus's original work)

3. Kerfoot BP, DeWolf WC, Masser BA, Church PA, Federman DD. Spaced education improves the retention of clinical knowledge by

medical students: a randomized controlled trial. *Med Educ.* 2007; 41(1): 23-31.

4. Spruit EN, Band GPH, Hamming JF. Increasing efficiency of surgical training: effects of spacing practice on skill acquisition and retention in laparoscopy training. *Surg Endosc.* 2015; 29(8): 2235-2243.

5. Rasch B, Born J. About sleep's role in memory. *Physiol Rev.* 2013; 93(2): 681-766.

CHAPTER 5

INTERLEAVING

Don't Be Afraid to Mix Things Up

If you're anything like I was as a student, you likely focus your studying efforts on a very narrow topic; hammering away until you feel like you have it down. I remember taking pride in my ability to focus on a very narrow topic for hours on end, only pausing when I needed more coffee. I'd take the same approach when trying to learn new clinical skills – never moving on until I could perform a skill without hesitation. Yet, somehow despite these heroic efforts, I still struggled to retain knowledge and often failed to see the bigger picture for the topics I was studying. In reality, my approach was far from optimal.

This approach of repeatedly reviewing a single topic (or repeatedly performing a clinical skill) is generally referred to as "blocking", since it essentially involves focusing on a single topic for a block of time. This is the approach that students often take for several reasons. First, it's entirely logical to focus on one topic or skill at a time, not moving on until feeling a sense of mastery – even if this turns out to be a false sense. Second, blocking tends to be perceived as highly effective, since it typically leads to noticeable improvements in our immediate performance (you will almost certainly become more familiar with your notes each time you cycle through them, which feels like progress). Finally, this is how information tends to be presented to learners. For instance, instructors often present topics in blocks, rarely revisiting previous concepts, since this is generally viewed as the student's responsibility. Textbooks and online tutorials are also organized in a similar manner – always building and moving forward, rarely revisiting concepts.

However, an alternative method referred to as *interleaving* has been shown to promote better learning outcomes when applied to various topics and in different contexts. Interleaving involves mixing up topics or skills. For example, consider a scenario where a student is studying three related topics (topics A, B, and C). Blocking would involve repeatedly reviewing topic A, then B, then C (e.g. AAABBBCCC). In contrast, interleaving would essentially involve bouncing from topic to topic (ABCABCABC). As an analogy, think of someone trying to work on their golf game. If using a blocked approach, their session may involve practice time spent putting, then chipping, and finally driving, likely not moving on from a type of shot until they've hit a few good ones in a row. With an interleaved approach, they would mix up the time they spent putting, chipping, and driving, moving between the three types of shots throughout their session (e.g. putting, then chipping, then driving, then returning for more putting).

At first, the interleaving approach probably seems nonsensical. It will also likely feel much more difficult since you'll need to frequently redirect your brain throughout a session (this turns out to be a good thing). However, there is emerging evidence that studying in an interleaved manner generally leads to better learning outcomes.

A LOOK AT THE LITERATURE

As we begin to consider the potential benefits of interleaving for learning, I'd like to highlight a study conducted by Drs. Nate Kornell and Robert Bjork, which was described in a paper published in the highly regarded journal, *Psychological Science*, back in 2008.[1]

Drs. Kornell and Bjork's study involved comparing college students' abilities to recognize the painting styles of 12 different artists. The students in their study viewed six different paintings from each artist. For six of the artists, the paintings were shown in a blocked manner. In other words, the students viewed all six paintings from a single artist consecutively, then viewed all six paintings from another artist, and so on. For the other six artists, the paintings were shown in an interleaved manner, with paintings from the different artists appearing in random order. After a short break, the students were presented with four new paintings from the same group of artists and asked to indicate which artist they thought painted each of them.

Kornell and Bjork's findings are shown in Figure 5.1. The students correctly identified the artist of the new paintings 35% of the time for the artists whose paintings they had viewed in a blocked manner, compared to 61% of the time for the artists whose paintings they had viewed in an interleaved manner. In other words, students performed better when the viewed paintings from a collection of artists in random order, compared to when they viewed all paintings from each artist consecutively.

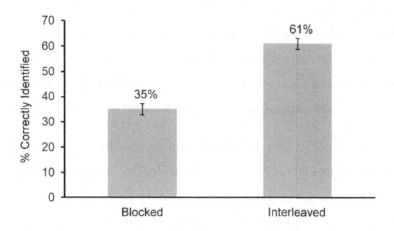

Figure 5.1. Mean (± standard error) percentage of artists correctly identified (% correctly identified) for paintings viewed in a blocked manner and interleaved manner.

What's interesting about the study by Drs. Kornell and Bjork is that their findings were exactly opposite of what they expected. They thought the blocked condition would result in a better ability to distinguish between the unique styles of different artists, since they believed consecutively viewing the paintings would help students pick up on subtle differences in the artists' styles – which turned out not to be the case.

Another interesting aspect of Drs. Kornell and Bjork's study is that they asked the students to predict which method would be better for learning the different artists' styles: blocked or interleaved. Surprisingly, the vast majority of the students thought that the blocked condition would lead to better performance, even though it ended up being far worse. Just another example of our minds deceiving us when it comes to optimal learning conditions.

Drs. Kornell and Bjork's work received significant attention after publication and has been cited over 800 times up to this point. That said, it could certainly be argued that recognizing portraits from different artists is of little relevance to health professions students. However, I'd argue that learning to identify the subtle details that can be used to distinguish between categories or conditions is often critical for healthcare providers.

As an example of how interleaving can be used by health professions students, let's consider the findings of a study by Dr. Anna Rozenshtein and her colleagues, which were described in a paper published in the *Journal of the American College of Radiology*.[2] Dr. Rozenshtein and her team wanted to compare a blocked approach and an interleaved approach for teaching medical students to identify different disorders when viewing chest X-rays.

They had their students view examples of 12 different radiographic patterns (e.g. emphysema, pneumonia, congestive heart failure), with six images for each pattern. Some students reviewed the images in a blocked manner, seeing all six images associated with a certain disease before moving to the next. Other students reviewed the images in an interleaved manner, seeing images from the different diseases in random order. After a short break, the students took a test where they were shown X-ray images and asked to identify the disease. Some of the images had been shown during the review period, while others were new images that the students hadn't seen yet.

Rozenshtein et al.'s findings are shown in Figure 5.2. For the images shown during the review period, the students who viewed the images in an interleaved manner correctly recalled the correct radiographic pattern 61% of the time, compared to only 47% of the time for those who viewed the images in a blocked manner. The results for the new images showed the same trend, with the interleaved group identifying the correct radiographic pattern 53% of the time, compared to only 40% of the time for the blocked group.

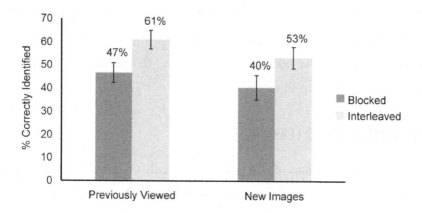

Figure 5.2. Mean (± standard error) percentage of radiographic patterns correctly identified (% correctly identified) by the students who viewed the images in a blocked manner (dark grey) vs. those who viewed the images in an interleaved manner (light grey), grouped according to whether the images had been previously viewed or not (new images).

These were important findings as they indicated that reviewing the images in an interleaved manner not only resulted in better recall, but also helped the medical students identify concerning radiographic patterns in previously unseen images, which is more reflective of what they'll need to do in clinical practice. Another win for interleaving!

BENEFITS BEYOND VISUAL RECOGNITION

So far, we've only discussed the benefits of interleaving for learning to visually distinguish between different types of images (e.g. identifying which artist painted a portrait or the specific disease present when viewing an X-ray). While interleaving can certainly be helpful in this context, the potential benefits extend more broadly, as there is evidence that interleaving can be beneficial for learning a wide range of concepts[3] and even more procedural skills like surgical techniques.[4] The knowledge gains produced by interleaving also tend to be longer-lasting, with less/slower forgetting. Emerging evidence also suggests that interleaving can help with higher-order processes like identifying common themes and summarizing information across multiple texts.

PARALLELS TO MOTOR LEARNING

Although the focus of this book is primarily on cognitive learning, it's interesting to consider the parallels with motor learning. Much like in cognitive learning, interleaving has been shown to be associated with superior outcomes in motor skill learning. For example, Drs. Sinah Goode and Richard Magill published a paper back in 1986, based on their study examining how practice ordering affected performance of three different badminton serves: the short serve, long serve, and drive serve.[5]

The subjects in their study, who were college students with no badminton experience, practiced each of the different types of serves. The students practiced three times per week, for three weeks. Some of them practiced in a blocked manner, performing a single type of serve during each session. Others practiced in an interleaved manner, performing all types of serves during each session, in a random order. Perhaps not surprisingly at this point in the chapter, the subjects who practiced in an interleaved manner exhibited better serve accuracy at the end of the three-week training period, compared to those who practiced in a blocked manner.

Again, these findings seem to parallel those from studies examining cognitive learning. It appears that scientists who studied motor learning were a bit ahead of those who studied cognitive learning when it came to understanding the potential benefits of interleaving.

WHY IS INTERLEAVING EFFECTIVE?

At this time, it isn't entirely clear why interleaving tends to be effective for promoting learning. However, one potential explanation is that it helps the brain develop the ability to differentiate between concepts or problem types, as learners need to continuously work to identify distinguishing features with each attempt. This is in contrast with blocking, where the mental work is largely done after the initial attempt since the subsequent problems will involve the same concept and general approach. Interleaving may also help to strengthen memory associations, since the more random nature requires frequent retrieval of information, which differs from blocking, where relevant information only needs to be retrieved once and then stored for short-term use until moving on to the next concept or problem type.

For example, consider a student completing a math practice problem set where the questions are arranged in a blocked manner. Once the student figures out the correct approach to solving the problem, they can simply apply the approach to the next problem (i.e. "plug-and-chug"), without needing to pause and consider what type of problem it is and possible approaches to solving it. However, if the questions were arranged in an interleaved manner (i.e. problem types mixed up), the student would need to work to identify the key features of each problem, consider different possible approaches, and retrieve relevant information from memory to solve it. This additional mental effort is the type of desirable difficulty that tends to produce robust learning outcomes. I've used learning math as an example here because this is an area where interleaving has shown great promise for students of all ages and levels.

HOW TO BUILD INTERLEAVING INTO YOUR ROUTINE

Now, let's consider a few ways that you can incorporate interleaving into your studying routine.

From my perspective, the biggest takeaway from this chapter should be to mix up the order of your studying. Students tend to study in a very linear manner, reviewing topics in the order they were presented. I think this is a missed opportunity to incorporate elements of interleaving.

For example, imagine you're studying for a physiology final exam. Instructors often organize physiology content based on the different organ systems of the body (skeletal, muscular, nervous, endocrine, cardiovascular, lymphatic, respiratory, digestive, urinary, reproductive), presenting each system as a separate unit. Textbooks and online tutorials are typically organized the same way. Therefore, students often review the organ systems as isolated units, focusing on a single system until they feel comfortable with it, then moving on to the next system.

While this approach seems logical, it may limit your ability to see the similarities and unique features of the different organ systems, and to appreciate how the systems must interact for the body to function optimally. A better approach may be to blend the topics together when studying (i.e. interleaving). For example, if you were working through practice questions as a form of review you could randomize the order so that questions pertaining to the different systems are mixed, instead of in blocks. This approach is also consistent with how most exams are organized (questions not grouped by topic or system), so it would be a good way to prepare for multiple reasons.

The same idea applies when learning to distinguish between different clinical presentations or to perform various clinical skills. For instance, imagine you're learning how to read and interpret an electrocardiogram, with the goal of being able to identify the general patterns associated with different types of heart arrhythmias. While you may opt to review multiple examples of each type arrythmia in a blocked manner, a better approach would be to interleave the examples of the different types of arrythmias during your review, so you can learn to differentiate between them. Or as another example, imagine you're learning to perform a skin cancer screening. Instead of repeatedly reviewing images of different types of cancerous lesions, it may be better to review images of a mix of cancerous and non-cancerous lesions so you can learn how to distinguish between them.

Interleaving may also be beneficial for learning to perform certain "hands-on" skills. For example, imagine you're a student physical therapist practicing different techniques to restore joint motion. You could focus on performing a specific technique repeatedly until you "have it down", then move on to the next technique and repeat the process (this was my [flawed] go-to approach). However, a better approach would likely be to blend practicing of the different techniques, since this will help you to identify the subtle differences between the techniques. Mixing up the practice order would also require more frequent recall, since you would need to retrieve information from your memory regarding hand positioning, patient positioning, and force application, with each attempt, not just when transitioning between the different techniques. Think about it, when you repeatedly practice a single technique (i.e. blocking) you really only need to go through the mental retrieval process once, which is a missed opportunity considering the positive learning outcomes associated with retrieval practice (discussed in Chapter 3).

Here are a couple final things to consider regarding interleaving. First, it's generally believed that interleaving will be most effective when concepts are at least somewhat related to each other. For example, you probably won't benefit much from interleaving topics from an anatomy class and a medical ethics class, since there likely isn't enough useful overlap between the concepts. Second, you likely need to have some knowledge of the topics for interleaving to be effective. If concepts are completely foreign to you, it may be hard for you to make connections. In general, I think interleaving works really well once you have at least a general understanding of the main concepts and ideas.

FINAL THOUGHTS

Although interleaving may not feel very natural (and can even be frustrating), it's a desirable difficulty that's worth building into your studying routine. I think interleaving is particularly important for health professions students to explore, since it's critical for healthcare providers to understand how concepts relate in order to see the entire picture of a patient's condition. Healthcare providers must also be able to identify the key signs, symptoms, etc. that differentiate one patient case from another. This is the type of higher-order processing that can be enhanced by using interleaving.

As is the case with all the techniques discussed in this book, you should feel free to be creative in how you incorporate interleaving into your routine. This chapter is just a starting point – the next step is for you to experiment with how to best put interleaving to use.

REFERENCES:

1. Kornell N, Bjork RA. Learning concepts and categories: is spacing the "enemy of induction." *Psychol Sci.* 2008; 19(6): 585-592.

2. Rozenshtein A, Pearson GDN, Yan SX, Liu AZ, Toy D. Effect of massed versus interleaved teaching method on performance of students in radiology. *J Am Coll Radiol.* 2016; 13(8): 979-984.

3. Firth J, Rivers I, Boyle J. A systematic review of interleaving as a concept learning strategy. *Rev Educ.* 2021; 9(2): 642-684.

4. Goldin SB, Horn GT, Schnaus MJ, et al. FLS skill acquisition: a comparison of blocked vs. interleaved practice. *J Surg Educ.* 2014; 71(4): 506-512.

5. Goode S, Magill RA. Contextual interference effects in learning three badminton serves. *Res Q Exerc Sport.* 1986; 57(4): 308-314.

CHAPTER 6:

ELABORATION

Working to Dig Deeper and Make Connections

As a student, I spent a lot of time reviewing my notes and reading (and re-reading) my textbook. I'd find a quiet, comfortable spot in the library and hunker down until I had read every word. It felt good when I finished reading a chapter or reviewing a section of my notes, since I assumed this time spent reading/re-reading would translate into more knowledge and better understanding. However, I found that I often didn't gain much from these sessions. My eyes would move from word-to-word, but what I read just didn't seem to stick in my mind. In most cases, I'd reach the end of a chapter or section of my notes and not be able to recall much of anything about what I had just read. Even highlighting or underlining key concepts didn't seem to help much.

The problem with my approach was that I wasn't really working to process the information I was reading/reviewing. It was passing through my brain, but I wasn't doing anything to make it stick. I've come to realize that as learners, we need to engage with information and concepts in order to have any shot at retaining them. This means taking the time to think, make connections, question, and so on. The more we mentally wrestle with the material, the better we'll understand it and the more likely we'll be to retain it. On the other hand, information we don't engage with tends to pass by, without leaving much of a trace.

The focus of this chapter is on *elaboration*, which involves working to develop a deeper understanding of a topic and attempting to make connections between new information and our prior knowledge, personal experiences, etc. These efforts to layer on additional levels of detail and to make connections can help to promote stronger and more lasting memories. Elaboration can also help you see the "bigger picture" of how concepts are related to one another.

Although the evidence supporting elaboration as a learning strategy isn't quite as strong as it is for things like retrieval practice and spaced practice, it can be a useful adjunct to these other strategies. Personally, I've found that elaboration helps me overcome my tendency to mindlessly breeze through materials.

A LOOK AT THE LITERATURE

As an example of the potential impact of elaboration, let's consider a study by Dr. Betty Lou Smith and her colleagues at Salisbury University.[1] Dr. Smith's team examined whether incorporating questioning during reading helps students comprehend challenging science texts.

As part of their study, Dr. Smith and her collaborators had college students enrolled in an introductory biology course read a chapter about the digestive system from a physiology textbook. The students were randomly assigned to either read the chapter twice (control group) or to read the chapter once, while pausing periodically to answer questions about what they had just read (experimental group). The questions prompted the students to think more deeply and to connect different concepts from the text. This strategy is generally referred to as "elaborative interrogation". It's discussed in more detail in the next section.

After reading the chapter (and re-reading in some cases), the students took a test based on what they had read about digestion. The students in the experimental group, who had answered questions periodically while reading the chapter, outperformed the students in the control group, who had simply read the chapter twice. In other words, incorporating questions that promoted elaboration throughout the text helped students remember and understand what they had read about the digestive system.

These findings from Dr. Smith and her colleagues indicate that stopping periodically to answer questions can help to promote better retention and understanding of a topic. You can make use of this strategy by pausing to ask yourself probing questions as you read or review your notes. We'll discuss other types of elaboration strategies in the next section.

HOW TO BUILD ELABORATION INTO YOUR ROUTINE

Now, let's discuss a few ways you can incorporate activities that involve elaboration into your studying routine.

Elaborative interrogation

Elaborative interrogation involves asking yourself questions as you read/review about how and why things work, similarities and differences between concepts, and so on. You then work to answer the questions you've generated, either by reviewing your materials or from memory. Elaborative interrogation has been studied extensively and appears to be effective for promoting recall and facilitating higher-level reasoning.[2-4]

The general idea behind elaborative interrogation is to use questioning to push yourself to think more deeply about a topic and to make connections between what you are trying to learn and your prior knowledge. It can also help you identify gaps in your understanding, as it's common to end up asking questions you aren't able to answer, especially when you first start studying a topic.

As an example, imagine that you're using elaborative interrogation when reading about the structure of veins. In this case, as you read you would pause to ask yourself questions like, *why do veins have valves?* Or, *how do veins differ from arteries in terms of their structure?* These types of questions would help you to associate isolated facts about the structure of veins to what you already know about the general functioning of the circulatory system. Not surprisingly, this will create a stronger memory and deeper level of understanding compared to simply moving your eyes over the words in your textbook or notes.

With elaborative interrogation, it's okay if you need to rely on notes, textbooks, or other course materials to answer your questions as you begin to learn about a topic. However, as you progress, you'll want to try answering your questions from memory, before reviewing your course materials to check the accuracy of your responses. This will allow you to incorporate some retrieval practice while also practicing elaboration. You can also try asking yourself different questions each time you review, so you continuously explore different aspects of a topic, essentially working to build upon your understanding over time.

Personally, I use elaborative interrogation quite often, especially when reading. If you look at any paper or book I've read you'll notice that the margins are filled with questions. I find that elaborative interrogation not only improves my reading comprehension and retention, but also makes reading more fun and engaging (which is probably part of why I tend to retain more). Chapter 10 includes additional information about how to effectively read for the purpose of learning.

Concept mapping

Concept mapping is also commonly used to promote elaboration.[5,6] Concept mapping involves creating a diagram ("concept map") where the relationships between concepts can be easily visualized. In a concept map, concepts are typically outlined in boxes or circles, referred to as "nodes", while lines/arrows and linking verbs are used to show how these concepts are related.

Concept mapping can help to provide structure and organization to how you conceptualize information related to a topic. It can also help you see the "bigger picture" of how concepts relate to one another.

A great thing about concept mapping is that you can continue to expand upon your map as you learn more about a topic. Your map essentially becomes a living diagram that reflects your evolving conceptual understanding.

It can also be helpful to talk a classmate through your concept map and then have them do the same for theirs. It's interesting and generally helpful to see how different people conceptualize and organize information and concepts related to a topic. Everyone's concept map will differ – and that's okay.

I also recommend attempting to create your concept map from memory (as much as possible), instead of relying on your notes or other course materials. This is a way to blend in an element of retrieval practice, which is generally good for learning. In fact, there is evidence to suggest that completing a concept map from memory tends to be better for learning, compared to when relying on notes or other course materials.[7]

I won't go into depth regarding concept mapping since it takes some practice and guidance to become effective with this technique. However, there are lots of helpful online tutorials available if you decide you want to make concept mapping a part of your studying routine. Again, I highly recommend it. A paper by Pintoi and Zeitz[8] also provides an excellent overview of how to get started with concept mapping (full reference at the end of the chapter). That said, I wouldn't be overly concerned with some of the subtle details regarding how to design a concept map. In my opinion the process of creating a concept map is what's most important, not the visual appeal of the final product (at least when you're making a concept map for learning purposes).

It's worth noting that there are software programs available to help you with creating concept maps. For example, Cmap is a very popular, free software program that's designed for creating concept maps (https://cmap.ihmc.us/). There are also other programs that offer similar functionality. However, any electronic document or slide will work. You can also create concept maps using paper, but it often becomes messy and disorganized pretty quickly, since you may not have a good idea of how concepts fit together initially. It usually takes some reorganizing, adjusting, and adding as you develop your concept map.

Creating analogies

An analogy is a comparison of two otherwise unlike things to highlight how they are similar in a certain regard. For example, consider the famous line, "life is like a box of chocolates, you never know what you're gonna get", from the movie Forrest Gump. In this case, Tom Hanks' character is associating two dissimilar things – life and a box of chocolates – based on the one characteristic they have in common – their unpredictability. I'm sure you've already encountered quite a few analogies up to this point in your education. Teachers, including me, tend to love analogies.

Analogies can be effective learning tools since they allow us to associate a new concept with something we already know, essentially linking new information with an existing memory framework. By creating this connection, we make it easier to both remember and retrieve what we are trying to learn.

As an example, in a paper published back in 2000, physiologist Dr. David Swain described how the cardiovascular system is analogous to a city water supply, where the heart functions as the pump, the aorta as the water tower, the arteries as distribution pipes, and the arterioles as faucets.[9] Dr. Swain's goal in creating this analogy was to help students connect what they are learning about the cardiovascular system to something they may be more familiar with.

I've also found that analogies can help students reason through questions they may not know off hand. For instance, imagine a student taking a physiology exam who is stumped by a question related to the cardiovascular system. Even if the student hadn't memorized the correct answer, they could consider the city water supply analogy and probably use logic to come up with a reasonable answer.

Analogies won't always be perfect; there are certainly some differences between the circulatory system and a city's water supply. However, they can be useful. So, the next time you're trying to learn something new, it may be worth asking yourself, *what does this remind me of?*

Again, these are just a few examples of how you can incorporate elaboration into your studying routine. There are certainly other options. Really anything that forces you to dig deeper and search for connections is worth your time and mental effort in my opinion.

WHY IS ELABORATION EFFECTIVE?

There are a lot of different ideas as to how elaboration may promote learning; however, here's how I conceptualize it. We don't generally store and retrieve isolated pieces of information in long-term memory. Instead, our brain creates elaborate, interconnected networks that organize and link related pieces of information together. As we've discussed, elaboration involves digging deeper, associating new information with what we already know, and connecting related concepts. Therefore, in theory, this should be helpful for adding to and expanding upon existing memory networks. Which in turn, should result in more efficient storage and retrieval of information. In other words, with elaboration we try to process information in a manner that will make it easier to store and then readily retrieve from memory. I like to think of it as helping our brain to logically organize all the information it's being bombarded with, so we can make use of it later.

FINAL THOUGHTS

The elaboration strategies outlined in this chapter can push you to continuously dig deeper, while also helping you to understand how concepts relate and the relevance of what you're learning. I think this is particularly important for healthcare providers, who must be able to see the "big picture", but also appreciate minor details (essentially seeing both the forest and the trees simultaneously). While this isn't easy, incorporating elaboration strategies can be helpful in this regard. Another tool in your study strategies toolbox.

REFERENCES:

1. Smith BL, Holliday WG, Austin HW. Students' comprehension of science textbooks using a question-based reading strategy. *JRST*. 2010; 47(4): 363-379.

2. McDaniel MA, Donnelly CM. Learning with analogy and elaborative interrogation. *J Educ Psychol*. 1996; 88(3): 508-519.

3. Pressley M, Symons S, McDaniel MA, Snyder BL, Turnure JE. Elaborative interrogation facilitates acquisition of confusing facts. *J Educ Psychol*. 1988; 80(3): 268-278.

4. Woloshyn VE, Willoughby T, Wood E, Pressley M. Elaborative interrogation facilitates learning of factual paragraphs. *J Educ Psychol*. 1990; 82(3): 513-524.

5. Brondfield S, Seol A, Hyland K, Teherani A, Hsu G. Integrating concept maps into a medical student oncology curriculum. *J Cancer Educ*. 2021; 36(1): 85-91.

6. Rendas AB, Fonseca M, Pinto PR. Toward meaningful learning in undergraduate medical education using concept maps in a PBL pathophysiology course. *Adv Physiol Educ*. 2006; 30(1): 23-29.

7. Blunt JR, Karpicke JD. Learning with retrieval-based concept mapping. *J Educ Psychol*. 2014; 106(3): 849-858.

8. Pintoi AJ, Zeitz HJ. Concept mapping: a strategy for promoting meaningful learning in medical education. *Med Teach*. 1997; 19(2): 114-121.

9. Swain DP. The water-tower analogy of the cardiovascular system. *Adv Physiol Educ*. 2000; 24(1): 43-50.

CHAPTER 7

CONCRETE EXAMPLES

Making Learning Come to Life

Like most instructors, I provide lots of examples in my classes. Especially when teaching abstract concepts, which are ideas that don't have a physical form (i.e. existing only in the mind). Because of their abstract nature, these types of concepts can be particularly hard for students to grasp. However, I've found that good, relatable examples can help students to understand abstract concepts. Examples can also help students see how what they're learning is relevant to their day-to-day life. Through examples we can essentially turn an abstract idea into something more concrete.

For instance, I recently gave a lecture on cognitive biases to my students. One of the biases I discussed was the so-called *confirmation bias*, which is the tendency for people to focus on information that fits their current beliefs and ignore information that doesn't. While the students may have been able to get the gist of what I was talking about from the definition, I used a real-life example to make the concept of confirmation bias more understandable and relatable. The example I gave was of a clinician examining a patient who had already been diagnosed with a certain condition by another healthcare provider. In this case, the clinician would tend to focus on clinical exam findings that fit the patient's prior diagnosis, while dismissing findings that don't (a specific type of confirmation bias referred to as *diagnostic momentum*). In other words, the clinician may fail to examine the patient with a "fresh pair of eyes". This example helped to turn the abstract concept of confirmation bias into something more concrete, relatable, and clearly relevant to my students.

Instructors also often make use of real-life examples when writing exam questions, especially in areas related to healthcare education, where application is so critical. For instance, when I wrote exam questions for the cognitive biases I discussed in my class, I didn't just provide the definition and ask my students to select the correct term from a list. Instead, I described a real-life scenario (such as the one from the last paragraph) and asked my students to select the specific type of cognitive bias it represented. My goal in writing these types of questions was to see if my students truly understood the concepts we discussed, or if they had simply memorized definitions. Getting used to linking concepts with examples will help you to answer these types of exam questions that require you to move beyond simply memorizing definitions and facts.

This chapter will focus on how *concrete examples* can be useful for learning abstract concepts. By concrete examples, I mean specific, real-life examples that you, as a learner, can connect with. These types of concrete examples can effectively create a bridge between something abstract and something more familiar and relatable. Learning from concrete examples will also help you answer those pesky exam questions that require you to move beyond memorization.

A LOOK AT THE LITERATURE

Most of the research examining the impact of concrete examples on learning has come from psychology (although concrete examples can be useful in many different contexts). For example, Dr. Katherine Rawson and her colleagues conducted a study to see if concrete examples help undergraduate students learn psychology concepts.[1] They published a paper based on their study in the journal, *Educational Psychology Review*, back in 2015. At the time, it was one of the first studies to rigorously examine the impact of concrete examples among college students.

For their study, Dr. Rawson and her colleagues had students review 10 different concepts related to the topic of human judgement and decision making. Some of the students were asked to repeatedly review the definitions of the concepts, while others read the definition and reviewed real-life examples of the different concepts. After a short break, the students were given new examples and asked to indicate which concept they represented, essentially matching examples to terms. Note that this is very similar to what instructors, including myself, often ask students to do on exams.

The students who studied concrete examples outperformed those who simply reviewed the definitions of the different concepts. These findings indicate that concrete examples can help students move beyond simply memorizing a definition, toward actually understanding the real-life applications of a concept. Dr. Rawson's team's findings have been replicated multiple times since their initial study.[2,3] At this point, there's certainly a well-establish body of literature supporting the use of concrete examples to promote learning.

So, studying concrete examples is good for learning abstract concepts, but what about generating your own examples? Dr. Rawson and Dr. John Dunlosky conducted a follow-up study addressing this question and found that student self-generated examples are also generally helpful for learning.[4] That said, they also found that the quality of the self-generated examples matters. Good examples support learning, but poor examples aren't that helpful. This is important to consider as you work to develop your own examples. We'll discuss this more later in the chapter.

WHY DO CONCRETE EXAMPLES PROMOTE LEARNING?

As I've already alluded to, it's typically harder to remember abstract concepts, since they aren't tangible by nature. We can make these concepts more concrete, and thus more relatable and memorable, if we associate them with real-life examples. In other words, we take an abstract idea and connect it to a situation that's easy for us to imagine.

Concrete examples can also help to motivate us to learn a concept, since they provide direct evidence of how what we're learning is relevant to our day-to-day lives. For instance, consider the example of confirmation bias I discussed earlier in the chapter, where the clinician was biased by having knowledge of a patient's prior diagnosis. I'm sure anyone training to become a healthcare provider could appreciate the potential consequences of this type of cognitive bias, as it's easy to imagine it leading to ongoing misdiagnosis, delayed or inappropriate treatment, patient frustration, and so on. Simply reviewing a definition of a concept isn't going to create this type of mental image.

HOW TO MAKE USE OF CONCRETE EXAMPLES

Now, let's discuss some tips for how to maximize the benefits of using concrete examples when studying.

Work to create your own examples

Your instructor will likely provide you with examples during class. You can also usually find examples online or in your textbook. However, it can also be helpful to generate your own examples, as this will push you to a higher level of Bloom's Taxonomy (generating an example reflects a higher level of learning compared to understanding one that's given to you).

One important caveat is to make sure that the examples you generate are accurate and complete, as there's evidence that students aren't always good at coming up with their own examples, especially when first learning a concept.[5] If possible, run the examples you come up with by your instructor to make sure they're accurate and complete. Most instructors will be happy to take the time to give you feedback if they see that you're putting in the time and effort to come up with your own examples.

Have multiple examples for each concept

It's good to have multiple examples for each concept you're trying to learn. Having multiple examples will help you appreciate different ways a concept can be applied. You'll also be able to see what the different examples have in common, making it easier to pick up on the key elements of a concept. If you truly understand a concept, you shouldn't be limited to one example.

Discuss examples with a classmate

Swapping examples with a classmate can be really helpful when learning a new concept. Just pick a concept, each generate an example, and then talk each other through the examples you came up with.

Hearing your classmate's examples can help to broaden your understanding of a concept, as they may think of applications or scenarios you'd never considered. This is also an opportunity for you to get feedback for the examples you came up with.

I do this as an in-class activity regularly and have found it to be very effective and fun for students. I'd consider adding this to your studying routine.

FINAL THOUGHTS

Of all the chapters in this book, this one is probably most intuitive. As learners, we naturally tend to seek out relatable examples whenever we're introduced to a new concept. As it turns out, this is a rare case where something we perceive to be helpful for our learning, actually turns out to be. So, by all means, seek out examples and make them a big part of your studying routine. I think you'll find that concepts stick better when they're more concrete.

REFERENCES:

1. Rawson KA, Thomas RC, Jacoby LL. The power of examples: illustrative examples enhance conceptual learning of declarative concepts. *Educ Psychol Rev*. 2015; 27(3): 483-504.

2. Micallef A, Newton PM. The use of concrete examples enhances the learning of abstract concepts; a replication study. *Teach Psychol.* 2022; 009862832110580.

3. Wissman KT, Zamary A, Rawson KA, Dunlosky J. Enhancing declarative concept application: the utility of examples as primary targets of learning. *J Exp Psychol Appl.* 2023; 29(2): 341-357.

4. Rawson KA, Dunlosky J. How effective is example generation for learning declarative concepts? *Educ Psychol Rev.* 2016; 28: 649-672.

5. Zamary A, Rawson KA, Dunlosky J. How accurately can students evaluate the quality of self-generated examples of declarative concepts? Not well, and feedback does not help. *Learn Instr.* 2016; 46: 12-20.

CHAPTER 8

DUAL CODING

Making Verbal-Visual Connections

As a student, I always needed good visuals to help me learn. I'd review my notes or read the textbook but felt like I couldn't fully grasp what I was reading unless I could see it in some way.

For example, if I was learning about the nervous system I would read about a structure or region, then look at my neuroanatomy atlas for a picture or illustration. Or if I read about how signals were sent and processed throughout the nervous system, I'd look for a diagram showing the connections and flow of information. I'd jump back and forth between reading text and looking at pictures or diagrams. To me, it felt like visuals helped me understand structure, general organization, and inter-connections, while reading allowed me to layer on additional details. This was one of my go-to approaches when I was studying. Especially for courses like anatomy and physiology, where it's critical to understand how complex systems are organized and how they work.

While I didn't always have the best study habits as a student, this is one thing I got right. There's a lot of evidence indicating that we learn best when reviewing information in both verbal and visual formats, such as reading text (verbal) and looking at a diagram (visual). By studying information in both verbal and visual forms we can create stronger and more elaborate memory structures.

The focus of this chapter is on *dual coding*, which is essentially the idea that learning can be enhanced by combining verbal (i.e. text, speech) and non-verbal representations of information. You may also hear this described as "multimodal learning", since it involves integrating information in multiple forms or modalities. In most cases dual coding involves pairing information in verbal and visual formats, such as text and diagrams. This approach of combining verbal and visual representations has been shown to improve knowledge retention and promote higher-level cognitive processes like problem solving.

A LOOK AT THE LITERATURE

As an example of how combining verbal and visual information can be used to support learning, let's consider a series of studies conducted by Drs. Richard Mayer and Joan Gallini.[1] Drs. Mayer and Gallini had undergraduate students read passages about how different devices work. The devices they had students learn about were brakes, pumps, and generators. While some of the students only read the passages (verbal only), others read while also viewing diagrams with labels of the system's parts and key steps in their actions (verbal and visual). These diagrams were intended to provide a visual representation of how the device functioned, by showing what was described in the text.

Students who viewed the diagrams, in addition to reading the passages, recalled more information about how the devices worked, compared to those who only read the passages. In addition, students who viewed the diagrams were also better at problem solving for the different devices. For instance, Drs. Mayer and Gallini asked students questions like, *"suppose that you press on the brake pedal in your car, but the brakes don't work. What could have gone wrong?"* Or, *"what could be done to make brakes more reliable?"* Students who viewed the diagrams were able to come up with more possible reasons or solutions to these questions that required problem solving, compared to those who only read. These findings indicate that presenting information both verbally (text) and visually (diagrams) promoted better understanding and creative problem solving.

While you're probably not learning about the workings of brakes, pumps, or generators, I'm sure you can imagine how Drs. Mayer and Gallini's findings could be relevant to healthcare providers, who need to understand how body systems work, what could cause them to stop working, and possible solutions if an issue arises. Interestingly, Dr. Mayer and Dr. Valerie Sims conducted a follow-up study and found that supplementing text with animations helped students learn about how the human respiratory system works and to problem solve different respiratory issues.[2] Understanding the functioning of the respiratory system is probably highly relevant to most of you who are reading this book.

THEORETICAL BASIS FOR DUAL CODING

The benefits of combining verbal and visual information for learning are likely related to how our brain processes and stores different types of information. In the early 1970's Dr. Allan Paivio proposed a "dual coding theory" to describe how the mind processes verbal information (e.g. text, speech) and non-verbal information (e.g. images).[3,4] According to dual coding theory, verbal and visual inputs are processed separately in our working memory by two distinct channels or systems. These systems function to create mental representations of the verbal and visual inputs. For example, when we read or hear the term "nose", our verbal processing system constructs a mental representation of the word. When we see a nose, our visual processing system constructs a mental image of a nose.

While verbal and visual information is processed separately, dual coding theory also proposes that there are connections between the verbal and visual systems (i.e. between-system connections). It's why reading or hearing the term "nose" can produce a mental image of a nose. Or, conversely, why seeing a picture of nose may help us come up with the word "nose". This connection between our verbal and visual systems is thought to be the basis for why combining information in verbal and visual forms (e.g. reading text and looking at a diagram) can be helpful for learning. If we can coordinate the processing of verbal information and visual information, we essentially create a more elaborate and inter-connected mental representation. In other words, we can effectively link verbal information with something visual, and vice versa. Figure 8.1 includes a simple diagram showing how information is processed according to dual coding theory.

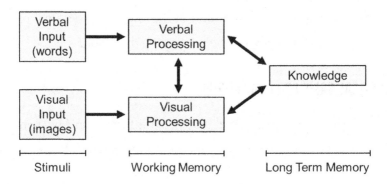

Figure 8.1. Diagram showing how verbal and visual information is processed by distinct, yet interconnected, systems or channels in our working memory, before being stored in long term memory.

Now, let's consider the example we discussed in the last section. Drs. Mayer and Gallini found that having students read text passages (verbal information) while also viewing diagrams (visual information) led to better knowledge retention and problem-solving abilities, compared to just reading the text (verbal information only). In the context of dual coding theory, this isn't surprising, since reading text and viewing related diagrams essentially creates a bridge between learners' verbal and visual systems.

Another interesting idea proposed as part of dual coding theory is that a verbal representation is linked to other related verbal representations. For example, reading the word "nose" may activate verbal representations for "smell" or "face". The same is true for visual representations (i.e. visualizing a nose may activate mental images of other facial features). You can think of these as connections within the two systems. This is another example of how our brain works to create elaborate inter-connections. It's important to study in a manner that facilitates these connections, as this will make it easier to retrieve information from memory and understand how concepts are related.

It should be noted that what I've outlined here is a very simplified overview of dual coding theory. Drs. James Clark and Allan Paivio's review paper[4] is a great place to start if you're interested in learning more about dual coding theory (I've included the reference at the end of this chapter). That said, my hope is that what I've outlined here is enough to drive home the point that there's a theoretical basis for the benefits of pairing verbal and visual information.

TIPS FOR MAXIMIZING THE BENEFITS OF DUAL CODING

Now, let's discuss some tips for how you can maximize the benefits of dual coding.

Study information in verbal and visual forms at the same time

To build verbal-visual connections, you should study information in verbal and visual forms at roughly the same time.[2] For instance, it would be better to move back and forth between reading text and viewing diagrams, instead of reading a full text, then moving on to review diagrams. Creating temporal alignment between the visual and verbal information helps to connect these modalities. I like to think of this as using visuals to build a framework and text to flesh out the details.

Rely heavily on visuals when first learning a topic

Drs. Mayer and Gallini's series of studies[1] examining the effects of pairing diagrams with text found that novice learners benefited a lot from visuals. However, visuals weren't that helpful for more experienced learners. In other words, students with little knowledge of brakes, pumps, or generators were helped a great deal by viewing diagrams, while the diagrams weren't very helpful for students who already knew quite a bit about these devices. Drs. Mayer and Gallini explained that more experienced learners likely already have well established mental models and therefore don't benefit as much from visuals. With this in mind, I would rely on visuals quite a bit as you're starting to learn about a topic but understand that they may become less critical once you've established a knowledge base.

Generate your own visuals

While it's great to rely on visuals from your instructor, the textbook, or other sources, it can also be helpful to generate your own visuals (as long as they're accurate).[5] As you read, try to sketch out diagrams showing the steps of a process or map out the connections among different concepts. You can use different formats for your visuals (e.g. diagrams, concept maps, infographics, timelines), depending on what you're trying to learn. Creating your own visuals will push you to a higher level of Bloom's Taxonomy. It can also be helpful to share and compare visuals with a classmate.

It's also important to note that "visuals" can also be in the form of physical models, cadaver prosections, and so on. Really anything that helps you create a mental visual representation that can be combined with verbal information. For example, if you are learning about the structure and function of the heart, you could combine reading from your textbook and studying a heart model.

WHAT DUAL CODING ISN'T

At first, dual coding probably sounds similar to the concept of "learning styles", which you may be familiar with – it's a popular, albeit flawed, concept. However, dual coding is quite different.

The general idea behind learning styles is that students have a specific way they learn best. For example, some may learn best from visuals, others from reading or listening. Based on this premise, it's commonly believed that learning can be maximized if students match the way they study to their learning style. For instance, based on the idea of individual learning styles a student who is a "visual learner" should use lots of visuals, while a student who is an "auditory learner" should rely more on listening or verbalizing ideas.

Despite the popularity of this idea of matching one's studying approaches to their learning style, there isn't good evidence to support this premise.[6,7] Studies have shown, quite convincingly, that while we may have ways we like to learn ("learning preferences"), this doesn't mean that this is how we learn best. In other words, so-called "visual learners" will not benefit more from visuals than so-called "auditory learners".

Dual coding isn't about matching modalities to learning styles or preferences. Instead, it's about processing information in different modalities or formats ("multimodal learning") and working to integrate these different sources of information. In essence, all learners should engage with information in different ways (read, visualize, listen, write, draw, etc.), regardless of what they prefer. While there isn't much evidence to support the idea of matching studying approaches to learning styles, there's plenty of evidence in support of dual coding for learning.

FINAL THOUGHTS

Effectively combining verbal information and visual information when studying can help you make connections you probably wouldn't make if you relied solely on one form or the other. By engaging with information in multiple formats, you can create the type of elaborate memory frameworks that are likely to stick and be useful as you begin to apply course concepts. In a sense, the adage that a *picture is worth a thousand words* turns out to be true when it comes to learning.

ONE MORE FINAL THOUGHT

I was on a flight to a conference as I was putting the finishing touches on this chapter. When I closed my laptop, I noticed the safety card in the seat back pocket in front of me. The card included a mix of text and pictures to explain what to do in case of an emergency. A great example of dual coding!

REFERENCES:

1. Mayer RE, Gallini JK. When is an illustration worth ten thousand words? *J Educ Psychol.* 1990; 82(4): 715-726.

2. Mayer RE, Sims VK. For whom is a picture worth a thousand words? Extensions of a dual-coding theory of multimodal learning. *J Educ Psychol.* 1994; 86(3): 389-401.

3. Paivio A. *Imagery and Verbal Processes.* Holt, Rinehart & Winston; 1971.

4. Clark JM, Paivio A. Dual coding theory and education. *Educ Psychol Rev.* 1991; 3(3): 149-210.

5. Hall VC, Bailey J, Tillman C. Can student-generated illustrations be worth ten thousand words? *J Educ Psychol.* 1997; 89(4): 677-681.

6. Newton PM, Najabat-Lattif HF, Santiago G, Salvi A. The learning styles neuromyth is still thriving in medical education. *Front Hum Neurosci.* 2021; 15: 708540.

7. Reiner C, Willingham D. The myth of learning styles. *Change: The Magazine of Higher Learning.* 2010; 42(5): 32-35.

CHAPTER 9

EFFECTIVE NOTE-TAKING

Taking useful notes during class can have a big impact on your learning. Good note-taking requires finding the right balance between trying to capture too much, or too little, of what's discussed. Students often try to record everything an instructor says during class, almost word-for-word. This type of verbatim note-taking generally isn't very effective, since you won't be able to process what's being covered and you'll likely miss the bigger picture by trying to record every minor detail. On the other hand, not taking sufficient notes can also be a problem since you won't have much to revisit when studying later. In the end, useful notes are those that capture the main points, along with some key details.

In this chapter, I'll introduce you to a note-taking approach referred to as the Cornell method, since it was developed by a professor at Cornell University named Dr. Walter Pauk.[1] While there are other note-taking approaches, each with their own strengths, I've found the Cornell method to be particularly useful, and many of my students have as well. In addition to being an effective way to organize notes, the Cornell method also encourages students to engage with their notes outside of class, which is critical for learning. In the end, taking good notes won't help you much if you don't revisit them later to review.

AN OVERVIEW OF THE CORNELL METHOD

When using the Cornell method, you typically divide your notes page into three sections: a notes area, a cue column, and a summary section. The notes area is located on the right side, taking up the largest portion of the page, while the cues column is on the left side of the page and the summary section is on the bottom of the page (Figure 9.1).

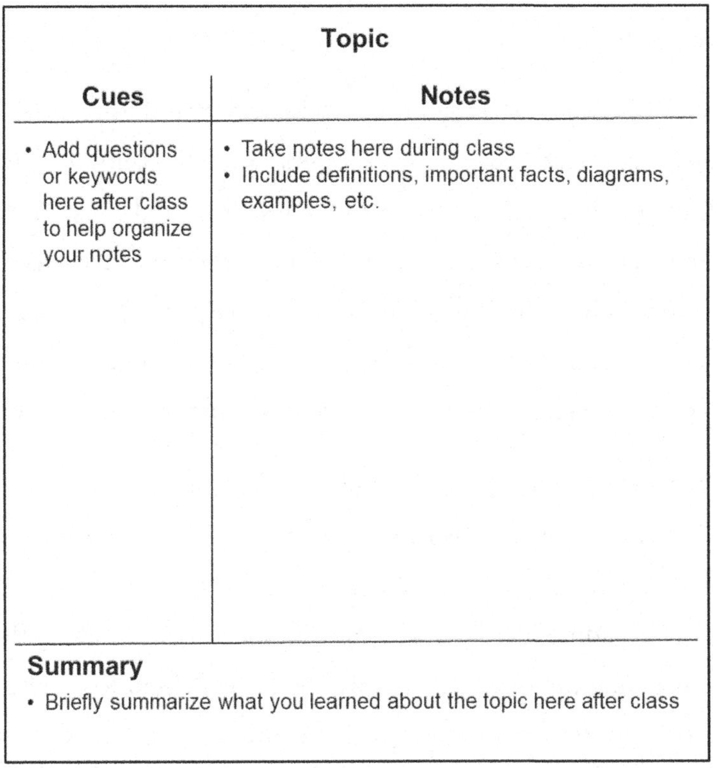

Topic	
Cues	**Notes**
• Add questions or keywords here after class to help organize your notes	• Take notes here during class • Include definitions, important facts, diagrams, examples, etc.

Summary
• Briefly summarize what you learned about the topic here after class

Figure 9.1. Typical page layout when taking notes using the Cornell method. The notes area is where you take notes during class, while the cues column and summary section are typically filled in after class.

Each section of the page serves a different purpose. The notes area is where you record information during class, while the cue column and summary section are usually filled in after class. Again, the Cornell method isn't just a format for in-class note-taking. Instead, it's more of a comprehensive note-taking process, where you take notes during class and then organize your notes and summarize main points after class.

Now, let's discuss the different sections of the notes page in greater detail.

The notes area

The notes area is where you record information during class, such as definitions, key facts, formulas, examples, and diagrams. For instance, imagine you're learning about cardiac physiology and your professor is discussing cardiac output. In your notes area you may record key information such as the definition of cardiac output, a list of factors that influence cardiac output, an equation for calculating cardiac output, and/or a diagram showing how different factors contribute to cardiac output.

When taking notes in class, use phrases to capture main ideas, instead of full sentences. You can also use abbreviations and symbols to improve efficiency, as long as you can remember what they mean later on when reviewing. Spending less time writing will allow more time for thinking. Simple diagrams and drawings can also be really helpful for showing how information is related, the steps in a process, and basic structural organization.

Again, you shouldn't try to record everything your instructor says word-for-word. Instead, focus on capturing the main points through paraphrasing, outlining, drawing, and so on. This type of note-taking involves a deeper level of cognitive processing (vs. trying to record everything verbatim), which will help you better understand the information being discussed. You can also write down questions that come up during class, so you can ask for clarification later. If you're coming up with questions during class, that's a good sign that you're actively processing the information at a level that's conducive to learning.

The cue column

The cue column is where you write questions or keywords that help to organize your notes, making it easier once you begin to review. What you are trying to do is group your notes into chunks of information. For example, for your notes related to cardiac output you may add the question *"what is cardiac output?"* or even just the keyword *"cardiac output"* in your cue column. These questions and/or keywords will give structure to your notes, essentially grouping related pieces of information.

The cue column is meant to be filled in shortly after class, while the information that was covered is still fresh in your mind. Revisiting your notes after class will allow you to identify points of confusion or possible gaps in your notes. Adding questions and/or keywords to the cue column also makes it easier to use your notes later when studying, as you'll be able to quickly scan through your notes to find specific subtopics.

The questions in the cue column can also serve as good prompts for retrieval practice. Just go through your notes and try to answer the questions in the cue column from memory and then check your notes to see if you could recall the key details discussed in class.

While it's generally recommended that you fill in the cue column after class, some students will fill it out during class, while they are also taking more detailed notes. Either approach can work well. That said, completing the cue column shortly after class forces you to revisit your notes, which is a good habit to get into.

The summary section

The summary section is where you briefly summarize what was discussed during class, in your own words. This section is usually limited to a few sentences or bullet points that provide a broad overview of the topic. By limiting yourself to a short summary, you're forced to reframe what you've learned through a broader lens. Like the cue column, it's best to complete the summary section shortly after class if possible.

While it's tempting to skip the summary, it's an important element of the Cornell method. Summarizing the main ideas from lecture can help you see the bigger picture, so you don't "miss the forest for the trees". It's easy to get lost in the details for classes with very dense content. I struggled with this at times as a student. I'd remember a lot of individual pieces of information but fail to see how they all fit together. Summarizing can help with this.

While the Cornell method of note-taking is fairly prescriptive regarding how to structure your notes and when to complete different sections, you should feel free to modify the approach as needed to fit your specific needs and preferences. In the end, the best note-taking approach is one that works well for you.

WHY YOU SHOULD CONSIDER THE CORNELL METHOD

Proponents of the Cornell method point out that it not only helps students to organize their notes, but also allows them to use their notes effectively as they begin to study. I've generally found this to be true, as

Cornell-style notes are easy to review and are conducive to retrieval practice, as students can attempt to recall details from memory based on questions or keywords included in their cue column.

The Cornell method also encourages students to revisit the notes they took during class, as they work to generate cues and summarize a topic. Revisiting your notes shortly after class is generally a good habit to get into.

The Cornell method can also work well outside of class when reading, watching videos, and so on. I personally use the Cornell method regularly for my own note-taking. I've found the structure and process of the Cornell method to be very effective for helping me organize and understand information. It's definitely worth trying out.

WRITING VS. TYPING YOUR NOTES

Students often take notes with a laptop. This raises the interesting question of whether it's better to take notes on a computer or by hand. Although this seems like a simple question, there isn't necessarily a clear answer at this time. There have been some studies suggesting that writing notes by hand is more beneficial for learning than taking notes via laptop.[2] However, the evidence isn't entirely clear at this point.

One of the potential drawbacks of taking notes with a laptop is that it makes it easier to record what's said in class verbatim, compared to taking notes by hand, since most people can type much faster than they can write. As a result, students who take notes with a computer often try to capture exactly what their instructor says word-for-word. In contrast, students taking notes by hand must paraphrase and focus on just the main points, since they can't write quickly enough to keep up with taking verbatim notes. This turns out to be advantageous, as having to take what's said and reframe it requires a deeper level of cognitive processing, which is generally good for learning. Taking written notes can also make it easier to quickly sketch out diagrams and simple drawings, which can also be really helpful when taking notes.

All things considered, in my opinion it's less about the note-taking medium (laptop vs. pen-and-paper) and more about how you take notes. A laptop (or other electronic device) can be fine, as long as you don't try to record everything your instructor says word-for-word (unless there's a specific reason to do so). If you're working to process and reframe what's being discussed in class, that's probably what matters, regardless of whether your notes end up in written or digital form.

One important caveat is that if you are using an electronic device to take notes, make sure you limit potential distractions, such as email or social media notifications. It can be tempting to check email or social media during class, but that can really detract from your learning. There will be plenty of time for those things once class is over or during breaks.

FINAL THOUGHTS

Taking good notes is important for optimizing your learning. While there are many different ways to take notes, the Cornell method is a very popular approach that can help you organize your notes and effectively study later on.

Regardless of how you take notes, it's important to take full advantage of your time spent in class by working to process information at a fairly deep level. Taking notes shouldn't just be viewed as a process of recording what's said in class. Instead, it's an opportunity to engage with the information being presented.

REFERENCES

1. Pauk W, Owens RJQ. *How to Study in College.* 11th ed. Cengage Learning; 2013.

2. Mueller PA, Oppenheimer DM. The pen is mightier than the keyboard: advantages of longhand over laptop note taking. *Psychol Sci.* 2014; 25(6): 1159-1168.

CHAPTER 10

HOW TO READ A TEXTBOOK

Instructors often encourage students to read the textbook. However, in my experience, very few students do. I can understand students' hesitancy toward spending time reading their textbook. As a student, I didn't always see the value in reading my textbook, or other course materials for that matter. It felt like reading took a lot of time, with little payoff when it came to my learning. What I've come to realize over the years is that I really didn't know how to read effectively. As I've become more effective at reading, I've come to appreciate how valuable a good textbook can be for learning.

To get the most out of reading your textbook, it's important to adopt an approach that will involve actively engaging with the content (generally referred to as "active reading"). Otherwise, you'll end up reaching the end of a chapter and remember very little of what you read. This was me as a student. My eyes would pass over the words, without really processing the information in the text. It's also important to consider your purpose for reading the textbook. Are you supplementing the information presented in class? Working to clarify specific points of confusion? Previewing for class? Whatever the reason, it's good to have a purpose in mind when reading your textbook, since your approach may vary depending on your purpose.

In this chapter, I'll discuss a few reasons to read your textbook and highlight some simple strategies you can use to get more out of the time you spend reading. When it comes to learning, a good textbook can be a very useful tool, as long as it's used effectively.

WHY YOU SHOULD READ YOUR TEXTBOOK

There are a number of a good reasons to read your textbook. One is that reading the textbook can supplement the information presented in class. During class, your goal should be to think about the information being presented and to take notes that capture the main points and key details so you can review later. That said, it can often feel like information overload, especially for dense courses like anatomy and physiology. Reading the textbook after class can help you fill gaps in your knowledge and solidify the main ideas discussed during class by layering on an additional level of detail.

Reading your textbook after class also gives you an opportunity to process information at a deeper level, since you control the pace when reading (i.e. you get to decide when to move on, unlike during class, where your instructor controls the pace). Sometimes it's hard to process information deeply during class since your instructor may move through topics quickly in order to cover everything in the allotted time. As a student, I always felt like I was frantically trying to keep up during lecture, with very little time to think. When reading, you'll be able to pause whenever you need to process the information you're trying to learn. This is your chance to think deeply, make connections, sketch out diagrams, come up with examples/analogies, and so on.

It's also worth noting that reading your textbook exposes you to a different way of conceptualizing information, since your instructor and the textbook author(s) will likely have unique ways of breaking down and presenting a topic. This unique perspective will broaden your level of understanding, helping you reach a higher level of knowledge mastery.

HOW TO READ A TEXTBOOK

There are lots of different approaches to reading a textbook. In this section I'll describe an approach that's worked well for me and many of my students.

First, take some time to preview the chapter before you begin reading. Scan the chapter headings and sub-headings, keywords, bolded terms, diagrams, and figures to get a sense of what you'll be reading about. It's tempting to skip this step, but it's good to start with an initial mental framework for what you'll be reading. This should only take a few minutes.

After you've previewed the chapter, you can begin reading. The key is to make sure you're actively processing the information in the text, otherwise you won't retain much. One way to do this is to stop to ask yourself questions as you read, using the *elaborative interrogation* approach introduced in Chapter 6. Building in questioning as you read will force you to pause to process the information in the chapter, which will help with retention and comprehension. You can also use the chapter headings and subheadings to generate questions. For example, if you're reading a section in your physiology book with the heading *"muscles of respiration"*, start by generating a simple question that you can attempt to answer through your reading such as, *what muscles are involved in respiration?* Then attempt to answer this question by reading the section. Having a specific question to address through your reading will help you stay focused while you read, as you'll be actively searching for the answer to your question. It can also be helpful to stop to summarize what you've read in your own words after each section, sub-section, or paragraph, depending on how dense the content is. These pauses to ask/answer questions and to summarize will help to prevent the type of "mindless reading" that's of little value for your learning (i.e. eyes moving across the page, with little cognitive processing).

It's also a good idea to take notes as you read, as this forces you to more fully attend to what you're reading. Like during lecture, don't try to write down everything word-for-word. Instead focus on the main points and reframe the information in your own words. If you have good notes from class, you can also compare the information from the textbook to what was presented during class. Ask yourself, which information is consistent? Which information appears to be inconsistent? Taking notes when reading also gives you something to quickly review later, since it's unlikely that you'll have the time to re-read large sections of your textbook.

Once you've reached the end of a chapter or section, use your notes to test yourself to see what you can recall from memory. Remember, attempting to recall information from memory is tremendously beneficial for learning (discussed in Chapter 3). You can also test yourself by attempting to answer questions at the end of the chapter if your textbook includes them (most do). After you've tested yourself, you can revisit sections of the text that are still unclear to you.

While this approach to reading takes time and lots of mental effort, it's worth it. While it's much quicker to move through the text without pausing to question, summarize, and take notes, you won't get much out of your time spent reading. Reading a textbook isn't like reading a novel, where you're reading for the purpose of entertainment. You need to actively engage with the textbook content if you want the information to stick. Since active reading requires focus and mental energy, be sure to take frequent breaks and divide your reading into manageable chunks. Don't feel like you need to read an entire chapter in one continuous session. Notice when your attention is starting to wander, or your mental energy is getting low, and take a break.

It's also worth noting that this approach can be applied when reading papers or other course materials, not just your textbook. I use this general approach whenever I'm reading for the sake of learning.

WHAT ABOUT HIGHLIGHTING?

Students often use highlighting (or underlining) when reading. While highlighting is popular among students, it generally isn't very helpful for learning, since it doesn't require you to deeply process what you're reading. Taking notes is a better way to extract key pieces of information from your textbook, especially if you translate the information into your own words and organize it into your own conceptual framework. While highlighting may be useful in some specific instances, it tends to be overutilized and can do more harm than good in some cases.

PREVIEWING BEFORE CLASS

In addition to reading after class, it can also be helpful to preview your textbook before class. When previewing, you don't need to read the chapter word-for-word. Instead, focus on the main ideas and bigger picture of what will be discussed during class. Start by looking over the chapter objectives, headings and sub-headings, keywords, bolded terms, and figures/diagrams. This initial scan of the chapter will help you get a general idea of what will be covered in class. It can also be helpful to read the chapter abstract or the end of chapter summary if available, as these sections provide a broad overview of the topic. Doing this type of previewing beforehand can help you take better notes and get more out of class, since your brain will be primed for what will be discussed. It's amazing how helpful it can be If you already have some familiarity with a topic prior to class. Then you can revisit your textbook after class to read more thoroughly. Again, this is how you can progressively layer on depth as you move from previewing before class, to processing during class, to diving into a greater level of detail after class. I like to think of previewing as dipping your toes into the water before eventually diving in!

FINAL THOUGHTS

Learning how to effectively utilize a textbook can make a big difference in your learning. The key is to adopt an active approach to reading that involves the type of cognitive processing that's conducive to meaningful learning. While it takes time and mental energy to effectively read a textbook, the payoff can be tremendous. So, don't just let your textbook collect dust on your shelf – open it and put it to good use.

CHAPTER 11

ADDITIONAL TIPS TO MAXIMIZE YOUR LEARNING

So far, I've described different evidence-based study strategies (Chapters 3-8), provided tips for taking useful notes (Chapter 9), and discussed how to effectively read a textbook or other course materials (Chapter 10). Using sound study strategies, taking good notes, and reading effectively will go a long way toward your academic success; however, these aren't the only ingredients for reaching your full learning potential.

In this chapter I'll focus on a few additional things you can do to maximize your learning and get the most out of your educational experience.

PREPARE FOR CLASS

Showing up to class on time, paying attention, and taking good notes are a must if you're going to be highly successful academically. That said, it's also important to do some upfront work so you can get the most out of your time in class. In my experience, most students don't take the time to adequately prepare for class. I equate this to trying to run a race without warming up first. You may still end up doing fine, but you won't maximize your performance. I think you'll find that preparing for class will allow you to be more engaged, take better notes, and generally feel less overwhelmed – sounds pretty good, right?

So, what do I mean by preparing for class? For starters, it's helpful to review what was covered in the last session before your next class, so you're ready to build on the information that was previously covered. Even 5-10 minutes of review can serve as a good refresher. Reviewing prior to class also helps you to identify points of confusion, so you can ask for clarification before the instructor moves on to the next topic.

In addition, it's also a good idea to preview what you'll be covering in class. You can preview by looking over your textbook chapter and/or lecture slides, or even by watching a short online video. When previewing, you're just trying to get a sense of what will be covered during class, as having some familiarity with the topic beforehand essentially primes your brain for what's coming. For example, let's say that you're scheduled to cover the *organization of the nervous system* in class. Before class you could spend some time previewing the textbook chapter on the topic. You don't need to read every word of the chapter. Just quickly look over the section headings/sub-headings, figures/diagrams, and bolded terms, and read the chapter summary to become familiar with the general topic. It can also be helpful to try answering the questions at the end of the chapter if your book has them, as there's evidence that attempting to answer questions beforehand can promote future learning (generally referred to as the "pretesting effect").[1] Don't worry if you can't answer the questions correctly; even unsuccessfully attempting to answer the questions prior to class can be helpful for your learning.

I'll admit, it probably seems a bit counterintuitive to spend time previewing before you've covered a topic. However, even 5-10 minutes of previewing can help to prepare your brain for what's going to be discussed in class. Again, I like to think of previewing as a sort of warm-up, so you're ready to get the most out of class. Students often find that it's easier to follow along in class and take notes if they already have some familiarity with the topic. Previewing can also help to prevent you from feeling overwhelmed during class. Students have told me that things seem to slow down a bit during class when they've done some prep work – it's certainly worth trying.

LEARN FROM EXAMS

Most students consider exams to be the bane of their existence. I get it – I hated taking exams. As a student, my goal was always to just get through an exam as quickly as possible so I could move on without looking back. I rarely took the time to thoroughly review my exams, which was a missed opportunity on my part.

I've come to realize that reviewing exams can be a tremendous learning opportunity. It's a chance to clarify any misconceptions and reinforce key concepts to promote retention (think of reviewing your exam as another study session). Remember, the goal isn't just to pass your exam and move on. You'll need to retain what you've learned to be successful in future courses and when you eventually start working with patients. As painful as it can be, don't miss out on the opportunity to learn from exams.

When reviewing your exam, go through each question, regardless of whether you got it right or wrong. Don't look at the answer key right away. See if you can still answer the question from memory after a few days have passed. If not, it's a sign that you should revisit the material. When you identify a point of confusion, ask your instructor to explain what makes a certain response option better than the others. Most instructors will be happy to spend time reviewing your exam, once they realize that you're interested in learning, not arguing about your score. Again, your learning doesn't need to end once you've finished the exam.

You can also look for patterns in the types of questions you got wrong, which can help you prepare better in the future. For example, you may find that you can correctly answer basic knowledge questions but struggle with questions that require application (which is very common). This provides some useful insights that you can use to adjust the way you study for future exams. If you begin to view exams as less of a hurdle to overcome and more of tool to support your learning, you'll get more out of your classes.

ESTABLISH AN EFFECTIVE STUDY GROUP

Establishing an effective study group is a must if you want to maximize your learning. Meeting with classmates to discuss course concepts can be extremely valuable. You'll learn a lot from hearing others' perspectives, as well as from sharing your own (remember, teaching others is a great way to learn). Study groups also provide opportunities to collectively engage in different active learning activities, such as concept mapping. In addition, your study group can serve as a source of support and accountability, helping you to stay motivated and on top of things in your classes.

That said, not all study groups are effective, and it can become easy to get sidetracked when studying with classmates. When establishing your study group, make sure you're working with peers who are as committed to learning as you are. You don't need to be close friends with the members of your study group. In fact, sometimes it can be harder to stay on-task when working with friends.[1] Your study group should be made up of people who will come to sessions prepared and ready to work. Again, these people may or may not be your close friends. It's usually best to limit your study group to five people at most (two or three is probably optimal). Otherwise, it can be difficult to keep everyone engaged and on task.

It's also important to set an agenda for each session. Your agenda should include what you'll focus on, what you plan to accomplish, approximately how long your session be, and what everyone should do ahead of time to prepare (e.g. review a certain topic, come up with questions, read the chapter). This will help to ensure that your sessions stay on track and are productive. It can also be helpful to select someone to facilitate each session. Everyone should contribute, but it can help to have someone designated to keep your sessions on track. Otherwise, it's easy for study sessions to become more about socializing (or venting in some cases). While it's important to socialize, you want to stay on task when you've designed time to study.

TAKE CARE OF YOURSELF PHYSICALLY AND MENTALLY

Using effective study strategies is critical for maximizing your learning. However, even the best study strategies won't be effective if you aren't taking care of yourself physically and mentally.

Training to become a healthcare professional is very challenging, both academically and non-academically. Unfortunately, students tend to

---

[1] I feel a bit like a hypocrite for telling you that it's sometimes best not to study with your friends. My wife and I got to know each other through a study group for a chemistry course we took as college freshmen. At this point, we've been married for over 10 years and have two kids. Life is funny sometimes. For the record, my wife got an A in the class, and I got a B. I guess she distracted me more than I distracted her.

neglect their personal health during their schooling, often adopting unhealthy eating habits, becoming more sedentary, and not getting enough sleep. I can personally attest to this. When I started graduate school to become a physical therapist, I didn't feel like I had the time to prepare healthy meals or exercise. I also sacrificed my sleep, routinely pulling late-night study sessions in an attempt to keep up with my courses. What I've come to realize is that by not prioritizing my own health and wellness, I limited myself as a learner. Taking the time to eat well, be physically active, and get adequate rest is crucial to learning.

As a busy student, I think it's important to be deliberate when it comes to your health behaviors. There's a lot biding for your time. If you don't set rules for yourself and explicitly schedule in time for things like physical activity, grocery shopping, meal preparation, and rest, you'll likely slip into a pattern where your schoolwork consumes you and starts to take its toll on your health and general wellbeing.

Here are a couple of things that worked for me as a student. First, I created a few rules I knew I could live by. For instance, I stopped studying after 10 PM. Even if I had an exam the next day, my studying stopped at that time – no exceptions. I made this rule because I started to realize that my late-night studying wasn't very productive. Also, this gave me some time to wind down before I went to sleep. I also started scheduling time in my day for physical activity. I found that if it was in my planner, I was more likely to follow through on my intentions to be physically active. Again, this time blocked to take care of my physical health was non-negotiable. Even if I felt like I didn't have time, I'd do it anyway. I noticed that even 20-30 minutes of physical activity gave me a boost in energy, helped to clear my head, and improved my sleep, which ultimately made me more productive when I studied (a win-win of sorts). I also started scheduling time for shopping, snack/meal preparation, laundry, and other necessary tasks. These changes I made weren't drastic and I still spent a lot of time studying, but my life felt more manageable once I became more deliberate about how I budgeted my time.

Coming up with a plan to help deal with the stresses associated with school is also critical. Anyone who's trained to become a healthcare professional understands how stressful school can be. For many students, this stress can begin to negatively impact their mental/physical health and academic performance. I don't pretend to have all the answers when it comes to effectively managing stress; this is an area I still find challenging personally. That said, a few things that I've found helpful are making sure I'm physically active every day (in nature if possible), getting a consistent and adequate amount of sleep, taking frequent mental breaks, and staying connected with friends and family. When I consistently do these things, I'm able to keep my stress at a manageable level and my mind functions better. When I don't, I notice that I tend to think less clearly and am less focused when I work.

I've also found mindfulness meditation to be helpful for managing stress. I didn't start meditating until fairly recently. However, I wish I had been more open to it as a student, as I've found that it's a great way to clear my head so I can focus on my work (or anything really). Now, I start all my writing sessions with some type of mindfulness practice. It's amazing how something as simple as focusing on your breathing for 5-10 minutes can help to focus your attention. I notice that mindfulness meditation helps to limit the types of distracting thoughts that can derail a study session (e.g. worrying about your never-ending to-do list). There's quite a bit of research indicating that mindfulness meditation and other types of mindfulness practices can help students to manage their stress and reduce their anxiety.[2,3,4] There are also studies demonstrating the neurophysiological basis for mindfulness interventions.[5] It's pretty amazing how something that's seemingly so simple can change brain activity patterns, and even brain structure. It's certainly worth trying to incorporate some type of mindfulness practice into your routine, especially if you feel like you're having trouble focusing when studying and dealing with the stresses of being a student. There are lots of great resources available if you're interested in getting started (e.g. online tutorials, apps, books).

Of course, it's also important to note that you should seek professional help if you are really struggling with your mental health. There are so many wonderful people who want to help you through whatever you're dealing with. Please don't try to do it alone.

Developing positive habits to take care of your physical and mental health as a student will also pay off in the longer-term, as you'll be able to carry these habits forward throughout your career. Being a healthcare provider can be stressful and physically/emotionally taxing. It's good to have a plan for dealing with these stresses and to try to prevent burnout. Starting to develop this plan as a student will help to ensure that you're ready to face the challenges of clinical practice.

FINAL THOUGHTS

Preparing for class, learning from exams (and other forms of assessment), establishing an effective study group, and taking care of your physical and mental health are key ingredients that make up a comprehensive plan to maximize your learning. If you combine these ingredients with effective study strategies, good note-taking, and active reading, you're on your way to being a highly successful learner.

REFERENCES:

1. Richland LE, Kornell N, Kao LS. The pretesting effect: do unsuccessful retrieval attempts enhance learning? *J Exp Psychol Appl.* 2009; 15(3): 243-257.

2. Burgstahler MS, Stenson MC. Effects of guided mindfulness meditation on anxiety and stress in a pre-healthcare college student population: a pilot study. *J Am Coll Health.* 2020; 68(6): 666-672.

3. Ross SJ, Owens K, Roberts A, Jennings E, Mylrea M. Mindfulness training: success in reducing first year health professional students' study and exam related stress. *Health Prof Educ.* 2020; 6: 162-169.

4. Kinser P, Braun S, Deeb G, Carrico C, Dow A. "Awareness if the first step": an interprofessional course on mindfulness & mindful-movement for healthcare professionals and students. *Complement Ther Clin Pract.* 2016; 25: 18-25.

5. Aly M, Ogasawara T, Kamijo K, Kojima H. Neurophysiological evidence of the transient beneficial effects of a brief mindfulness exercise on cognitive processing in young adults: an ERP study. *Mindfulness.* 2023; 14: 1102-1112.

6. Morais P, Quaresma C, Vigario R, Quintao C. Electrophysiological effects of mindfulness meditation in a concentration test. *Med Biol Eng Comput.* 2021; 59(4): 759-773.

CHAPTER 12

PUTTING IT ALL TOGETHER

Up to this point, I've introduced you to what I consider to be some of the key ingredients for academic success. Now, let's consider how these ingredients can be blended together into a comprehensive plan.

Imagine a student, let's call her Grace, who is training to become a healthcare provider. During her first semester, Grace takes a physiology course. Now, let's try to imagine how Grace could put some of the ideas discussed in this book into action for her physiology course.

At the start of the semester, Grace reviews the course objectives in the syllabus to get a general idea of what topics will be covered and the level she's expected reach by the end of the course. She notices that the course objectives tend to include action verbs like *apply*, *differentiate*, *relate*, and *appraise*. This is a signal to Grace that she will be expected to move beyond memorization and a basic understanding of concepts, to higher-level learning outcomes. Grace also notices that her instructor has broken the course down into sections based on the different body systems, with specific objectives for each section. She realizes that the section objectives will be useful for directing her studying.

As the semester begins, Grace gets into a routine for her physiology course. Her instructor primarily uses class time for lecture. Grace prepares for class by previewing the textbook chapter and reviewing the section objectives for the topic they'll be covering in class. During class she focuses on understanding the main points of what's being presented and takes notes so she can review later. Grace uses the Cornell method of note-taking, writing down key details in the notes area of her page. After class, Grace goes for a walk around campus for a mental break. Then she revisits her notes, completing the cue column and summary section.

That evening, Grace starts studying what was covered in class earlier in the day. She begins by attempting to answer the questions in the cue column of her notes from memory, and then reviews the notes area to check her answers. After she's reviewed her notes, she starts to read her textbook. As she reads, she pauses to ask questions and to check to see if the information in the textbook chapter is consistent with her class notes. She also supplements the notes she took in class with notes from her reading, using different colored ink to differentiate the two. Grace also carefully looks over the figures and diagrams in the textbook, and even takes time to sketch out some of them in her notes.

After she's done reading, Grace takes a short break and then begins reviewing a topic covered a couple weeks ago. She reviews by looking back over her notes on the topic, attempting to answer the questions in the cue column from memory and then checking the notes area to confirm that her answer is accurate and complete. Grace has already reviewed this topic multiple times at this point, so she doesn't need to rely on her notes much anymore. Grace takes this as a sign that she doesn't need to revisit this topic again until she begins final preparation for her exam.

The next morning, Grace wakes up, gets ready for her day, and then quickly reviews the topic covered in class the day prior. She reviews by attempting to write out what she can remember on a blank piece of paper and then looks at her notes to fill in missing details and to clarify points of confusion. Grace finds that she remembers more than she did last night – it's amazing what sleep can do for your memory. However, there are still things she's forgotten, so she plans to revisit the topic again in the next couple of days.

Grace continues this cycle of focusing on new material, while also making time to review older material periodically. She uses a planner to record when she's reviewed different topics, so she can keep track of when she should revisit them. Grace knows that the best way to avoid needing to cram is to carefully divide her time between learning new material and reviewing older material.

As her first physiology exam nears, Grace starts to change up her routine a bit. Her instructor has already covered everything that will be on the exam, so Grace is able to focus on reviewing material she's already studied, without needing to spend as much time learning new material. To review, Grace uses the section objectives provided by her instructor. She reframes each objective into a question and attempts to answer from memory. Then, she reviews her notes to make sure her response is accurate and complete. Grace mixes up the order in which she reviews the objectives, so that she interleaves questions related to the different body systems. Grace also takes a practice exam she found online. This gives her a chance to apply her knowledge to answer the types of questions that will be on her physiology exam. The practice exam also helps her to identify remaining gaps in her knowledge.

A few days before her exam, Grace meets with a classmate to study together. During the session, they decide to review some of the key physiologic processes covered in class. When reviewing, Grace and her classmate take turns explaining and sketching out a diagram of the steps involved in the different processes, while the other person ask questions and adds missing details as needed. After reviewing a process, Grace and her classmate try to come up with different problems that could arise and make predictions about how the body would likely respond. This pushes them to consider how the different components of the body systems interact and function together. At the end of the session, Grace and her classmate make a plan to meet with their instructor to ask a few questions that came up during their review session.

FINAL THOUGHTS

What I've presented here isn't an exact blueprint to follow. Instead, it's an example of what a comprehensive plan for academic success *can* look like for an individual class. Your plan will probably differ from Grace's, depending on your circumstances and preferences. Regardless, I think it's helpful to see how you can blend many of the different strategies and tips discussed throughout this book.

As you can see, it takes lots of diligence and careful planning to maximize your learning. I wish it were easy, but there really aren't any tricks or shortcuts that will beat hard work and a solid plan. That said, I'm confident that you can be successful with the right mindset and by applying some of the ideas outlined in this book.

AFTERWORD

As I reached the end of writing this book, I reflected on why the topic of learning is so important to me. In the end, I think it comes down to the high value I place on learning. In my opinion, there's nothing more transformational than "learning how to learn". Once you've learned how to learn, there's really nothing that can stop you from expanding your knowledge and skills – you're in control. It's empowering when you come to realize that if you work hard and take the right approach, you can learn anything.

I've personally experienced the power of learning how to learn. When I started college, I saw it as a means of getting a good job and a path toward a comfortable life, certainly not the transformational experience it became. During my educational journey I fell in love with learning (which is ultimately why I ended up staying in academia). It didn't happen in a single moment, and it wasn't because of a single person – I've been lucky to have many supporters and great coaches along the way. Instead, it occurred gradually. Every time I learned something new, it gave me confidence that I could be successful, as long as I worked hard and used the right approach. I took little steps forward and slowly began to see new challenges as opportunities for growth, instead of potential indictments of my intelligence. Every attempt at learning helped me refine my approach, regardless of whether I was successful or not. I continue this process of refining my approach to this day, as I push myself to learn new things and explore new topics.

When students struggle, they often believe it's because they aren't smart enough. It's easy to get into this mindset, especially when you're facing significant challenges and attempting to learn difficult things. I struggled with self-confidence when I first started college, and again when I started graduate school. I felt like an imposter of sorts. The one student who didn't belong, surrounded by people who were more intelligent and qualified than I was. What I've come to find out is that most students feel this way. My classes are filled with highly intelligent, motivated, hard-working students, who (wrongly) view themselves as inadequate. I've made it my mission to help these students be successful, so that they can begin to understand that they are capable of great things. That's really what this book is all about: helping students learn how to learn so they can experience the same type of transformation I did. To me, there's nothing more powerful than realizing that you're capable of learning anything.

As you can see, this topic is personal to me. I hope this came through in my writing. If this book helps even one person to reach their full potential, it will have been worth the time and energy I devoted to writing it.

Made in the USA
Las Vegas, NV
09 February 2024

85494973R00066